# ENGLISH DR

Series E
Bruce King

Tub
4.-P

ENGLISH DRAMATISTS
Series Editor: Bruce King

## Published titles

Richard Cave, *Ben Jonson*
Christine Richardson and Jackie Johnston, *Medieval Drama*
Roger Sales, *Christopher Marlowe*
Martin White, *Middleton and Tourneur*
Katharine Worth, *Sheridan and Goldsmith*

## Forthcoming titles

Susan Bassnett, *Shakespeare: Elizabethan Plays*
- John Bull, *Vanbrugh and Farquarson*
Barbara Kachur, *Etheridge and Wycherley*
Philip McGuire, *Shakespeare: Jacobean Plays*
— Kate McKluskie, *Dekker and Heywood*
Max Novak, *Fielding and Gay*
David Thomas, *William Congreve*
Cheryl Turner, *Early Women Dramatists*
Rowland Wymer, *Webster and Ford*

# MIDDLETON AND TOURNEUR

## Martin White

*Senior Lecturer in Drama at the University of Bristol*

MACMILLAN

First published 1992 by
THE MACMILLAN PRESS LTD
Houndmills, Basingstoke, Hampshire RG21 2XS
and London
Companies and representatives
throughout the world

ISBN 0–333–44066–8 hardcover
ISBN 0–333–44067–6 paperback

A catalogue record for this book is available
from the British Library.

Typeset by Nick Allen/Longworth Editorial Services
Longworth, Oxon.

Printed in Hong Kong

# Contents

# List of Illustrations

vii

*For Alison*

Now be your own judge: at your leisure look on it, at your pleasure laugh at it; and if you be sorry it is no better, you may be glad it is no bigger.

William Rowley, dedication to *A Fair Quarrel*

# Editor's Preface

Each generation needs to be introduced to the culture and great works of the past and to reinterpret them in its own ways. This series re-examines the important English dramatists of earlier centuries in the light of new information, new interests and new attitudes. The books are written for students, theatre-goers and general readers who want an up-to-date view of the plays and dramatists, with emphasis on drama as theatre and on stage, social and political history. Attention is given to what is known about performance, acting styles, changing interpretations, the stages and theatres of the time and theatre economics. The books will be relevant to those interested in or studying literature, theatre and cultural history.

BRUCE KING

# Preface

Thomas Middleton is best known for a reasonably small number of plays, of which his two late tragedies *Women Beware Women* and *The Changeling* are probably the most famous. His total output however, writing alone or in collaboration, was considerable, although a number of plays have not survived. Exactly how much he produced is a matter of speculation since there is a degree of uncertainty and disagreement over the authorship of some plays.

The most significant (and most written about) of the disputed attributions is that of *The Revenger's Tragedy*, but that of other works, such as *The Second Maiden's Tragedy* (which I believe to be Middleton's) and *Blurt, Master Constable* (which I do not) is also debated. Since space in this study is limited I have largely confined myself to those plays generally agreed to be Middleton's, but I have listed all works with which Middleton may definitely or possibly be associated in Appendix II.

# Acknowledgements

I am grateful to my friend and colleague John Marshall for willingly sharing his knowledge and ideas with me, and to Alison Steele for her willingness to listen patiently to countless outlines of arguments and to read and discuss numerous drafts of those arguments on paper.

I thank too those successive generations of students whose interest in these playwrights and participation in discussion, practical classes and productions have enabled me to develop my own thoughts. Many of the ideas that follow are undoubtedly theirs in origin; any errors, however, are entirely mine. I am especially grateful to those students who were involved in my production of *The Second Maiden's Tragedy* in 1988 and in the associated seminars, a combination that enabled me to test out ideas in practice and theory.

MARTIN WHITE

# 1
# Middleton's Early Work

*We are comedians, tragedians, tragi-comedians, comi-tragedians, pastorists, humourists, clownists, satirists: we have them, sir, from the hug to the smile, from the smile to the laugh, from the laugh to the handkerchief.*
*(Hengist, King of Kent, V. i)*

Thomas Middleton began to write for the stage sometime around 1602, and produced his last play – *A Game at Chess* – in 1624. His career therefore spans the Jacobean period almost exactly, and during that time he was involved in virtually every activity open to the professional playwright. He wrote for public and private theatres, adult and children's companies, pageants for the streets, entertainments for the court, and produced a range of work remarkable for its variety – and its quality.

He was born in London in 1580 and died there in 1627, and it is the values, inhabitants and environment of the city that provided the subject-matter, characters and settings for much of his work, including that set ostensibly in foreign locations or periods other than his own.

His father, William Middleton, a builder who became prosperous in the rapidly expanding capital, died when Thomas was nearly six years old and his sister, Avis, nearly four. William's widow, Anne (née Snow), soon remarried, but her relationship with her new husband, Thomas Harvey ('a Citizen and Grocer of London' as Middleton described him in 1600) was a tempestuous one, with much wrangling, quarrelling and litigation over money and property. One cannot know, of course, in what ways (if any) Middleton was affected or influenced by these events, but in the various dealings between his parents and other members of his immediate family: 'Trickery and chicanery seem to have been accepted as legitimate weapons, sometimes trickery of the rather improbable sort afterwards represented in Middleton's comedies' (Barker, 1958: 3).

Even though the lively events at home might have provided material for an aspiring writer, it may still have come as something of a relief to Thomas when, in 1598, he entered Queen's College, Oxford. Nothing much is known of his university career, though it seems he was short of money since he sold his share in some property he had inherited from his father in order to cover the money 'disbursed for my advauncement and preferment in the University of Oxford where I am nowe a studient and for my maintenance with meat drinke and apparell and other necessaries'.[1]

Middleton was perhaps recalling his own experience when, in his prose satire *Father Hubbard's Tales* (1604), he tells the story of a young man, not very well-off, who goes:

> like a poor scholar, to the university, not on horseback, but in Hobson's waggon, and all my pack contained in less than a little hood-box, my books not above four in number, and those four were very needful ones too, or else they had never been bought.  (101–2)[2]

Before long, the student is seduced away from his legitimate studies by other activities – in this case, writing poetry:

> I was unfruitfully led to the lickerish study of poetry, that sweet honey-poison, that swells a false scholar with unprofitable sweetness and delicious false conceits, until he burst into extremities, and become a poetical almsman, or at the most, one of the Poor Knights of Poetry.  (104)

The budding poet's first effort is 'an elaborate poetical building' (107), not unlike Middleton's own earliest work, *The Wisdom of Solomon Paraphrased* (from the Calvinist Geneva Bible version of the apocryphal books) – 700 six-line stanzas of 'adolescent jerks and flowers' (Shand, 1983: 67) – which appeared some time between March and December 1597, before he went to Oxford. Significantly, the poem is dedicated to the Earl of Essex, who had succeeded the Earl of Leicester as Elizabeth's favourite and who continued Leicester's support for the Puritans, which gives an early indication of Middleton's own religious and political sympathies.[3] Indeed, G. B. Shand has argued that dull as it is, the poem 'is the logical first step towards a major part of the mature career', with Middleton's aim being (if imperfectly realised): 'a statement of patriotic Elizabethan protestantism, Calvinistically tinged, and including much apparent compliment to Elizabeth herself' (Shand, 1983: 75).

While at Oxford Middleton published two further poems. *Micro-Cynicon*, a sequence of six 'Snarling Satyres' in which he attacked figures representing vices such as Prodigality and Lust, appeared in 1599, and anticipates the portrayal of a society brutalised by greed found in much of his comic and serious drama. Satire IV, for example, 'Cheating Drone', recounts the tricking of a 'silly gentleman' by a 'cheater' who 'takes more shapes than the chameleon', a story and characters similar to many found in cony-catching pamphlets and Middleton's own city comedies (see chapter 2). A year later he published *The Ghost of Lucrece*, clearly inspired and influenced by Shakespeare's poem, *The Rape of Lucrece*. It takes the form of a monologue by Lucrece's ghost on the dangers and violence of sexual depravity, in which she calls for revenge on Tarquin who raped her and drove her to suicide, themes that also figure strongly in Middleton's plays.[4]

## II

It is not clear whether he actually graduated or not, since in February 1601, around the time he should have been finishing his studies at Oxford, a legal document notes that Middleton 'nowe remaynethe heare in London daylie accompaninge the players', a phrase that is tantalisingly vague but which 'seems to mean that he was doing something more than just seeing plays day after day' (Barker, 1958: 8). It also seems likely that one of the results of this association with the players was an introduction to Mary Marbeck, one of whose brothers was an actor with the Admiral's Men, and who Middleton married at about this time. Mary came from a more distinguished family than his own, and one with long-standing Calvinist associations: indeed, her paternal grandfather, John Marbeck, a celebrated musician, had been tried in 1544 for his heretical views. Whether Middleton's marriage was calmer than his mother's to Thomas Harvey is not known: apart from the fact that Mary and he had a son, Edward, who was born in 1603 or 1604, and who was still alive twenty years later (he appeared before the Privy Council following the scandal over *A Game at Chess*), and that Mary died a year after Thomas, nothing is known of their life together.


## III


In 1603, with the playhouses temporarily closed due to the plague, and with the Bishops' Order of 1 June 1599, which had banned verse satires and epigrams, still in force (*Micro-Cynicon* had been among the works called in under the Order and burned by the public hangman), Middleton turned to prose. He wrote two satirical pamphlets – *Father Hubbard's Tales* and *The Black Book*, both published in 1604 – which in their style and viewpoint have an important bearing on his dramatic work.[5]

*Father Hubbard's Tales* consists of three stories told by an ant who has lived previous lives as various human beings (the third being the scholar's tale referred to above). The first story, 'The Ant's Tale when he was a ploughman', recounts the 'prodigal downfall' of a 'young landlord' who, having inherited his father's estate, mortgages his land and tenant workers to 'a lawyer, a mercer, and a merchant' in order to indulge in 'wild and unfruitful company about the court and London'. The cozening of the young heir is, significantly, told from the point of view of the suffering tenants, who stress the 'difference between the sweat of a ploughman and the sweat of a gentleman' (73).

The second story tells of the Ant's experiences as a soldier. It includes a story of a wife and a bawd collaborating to cozen the woman's husband (similar to the Harebrain plot in *A Mad World My Masters*), but concentrates on the plight of a man who loses his right arm and leg in a battle and who, on returning to England, finds himself laughed at for his deformity. As with the ploughman's story, this is also told from the point of view of the underdog, and Middleton expresses bitterly the injustice of the soldier's fate:

> Is this the farthest reward for a soldier? is valour and resolution, the two champions of the soul, so lightly esteemed and so basely undervalued? doth reeling Fortune not only rob us of our limbs, but of our living? are soldiers, then, food for cannon and for misery? (99)

The second of these prose satires, *The Black Book*, was intended by Middleton to 'bare the infectious bulks [bodies] of craft, cozenage, and panderism' (6) in London. Adopting a series of disguises (similar to those employed by the tricksters in *Michaelmas Term*), the Devil journeys round London, identifying and characterising its villains (brothel-keepers, landlords, dice-players, usurers, 'lusty vaulting gallants' with their 'spangled damnations') and visiting their haunts such as St Paul's 'to see fashions, to dive into villainous meetings, pernicious plots, black humours, and a million mischiefs, which are bred in that Cathedral womb' (32).

*The Black Book* concludes with Lucifer's will – 'the last Will and Testament of Lawrence Lucifer, the old wealthy bachelor of Limbo, alias Dick Devil-barn, the griping farmer of Kent' (33). Those who receive his bequests could be the characters in a city comedy, and display Middleton's characteristic flair for names – Benedick Bottomless, 'most deep cutpurse' (41), Francis Fingerfalse the dice-player, or Barnaby Burning-glass, 'arch-tobacco-taker of England' (42), and so on. But into the picaresque exhuberance of this satirical portrait is woven the acerbic criticism that one finds throughout Middleton's work, and with sharp and cynical irony lieutenant Prigbeard ('archpander of England' and the first to be remembered in the Will), is exhorted not only to 'dive . . . into landed novices' to get hold of their land, but to 'Let no young wriggle-eyed damosel, if her years have struck twelve once, be left unassaulted' (35).

Although not always recognised as such (Samuel Schoenbaum, for example dismisses it as 'exasperating juvenilia' – 1959: 287), Middleton's early prose and poetry is important for a proper understanding of his work overall. It indicates that while in his subsequent career as a professional playwright he was necessarily responsive to changing fashions in dramatic forms and audience tastes, his view of the world and those aspects of it that clearly engaged him and that recur throughout his work are evident from the very beginning of his career.


## IV

Middleton's earliest work for the stage has been lost. In 1602 he is named five times in Philip Henslowe's *Diary*, which is not in fact a journal but the account book of the Admiral's Men and Worcester's Men, theatre companies run by Henslowe, and based at the Rose playhouse, which had opened on the south bank of the Thames in 1587, and at the Fortune, built in 1600 in the suburbs about a mile north of St Paul's.[6] Among the works for which Henslowe paid Middleton was a play – now lost – called *Caesar's Fall* (with the rather bewildering alternative title, *Two Shapes*), which he wrote with Dekker, Drayton, Webster and Munday. Such multiple collaborations were not unusual in the period, and throughout his career Middleton continued to work with other writers, sharing contributions to the finished play in varying proportions. The same year, 1602, he received a total of £6 for a solo effort (also lost, or never printed) called *The Chester Tragedy, or, Randal Earl of Chester*, and in December he was paid 5 shillings for contributing a Prologue and Epilogue for a court performance of Robert Greene's *Friar Bacon and Friar Bungay*.

These early experiences – working collaboratively, writing alone, and contributing odds and ends to order as the company required them – provided Middleton with a grounding in the skills required by a professional dramatist, and remained his working pattern throughout his career.

## V

The first extant play that can be definitely attributed to Middleton alone is *The Phoenix*, a comedy, printed in 1607 but most probably written sometime in 1603–4. According to the title-page of the 1607 Quarto (which did not name Middleton as author; the attribution was first made in 1661 but is not disputed), it was 'sundrye times Acted by the Children of Paules', and it was by working for this theatre company in particular (though not exclusively) that Middleton began to establish himself as a writer. It seems likely that he began to write for them in 1603–4, and he soon became their leading dramatist, a position he maintained until the company ceased playing on a regular basis, apparently some time in 1606, before closing completely in 1608, and becoming the choristers 'singing school' (Gair, 1982: 173–4).

The Children of Paul's was one of two companies of boy actors then operating in London, the other being the Children of the Queen's Revels (formerly the Chapel Children) at the Blackfriars, to whom Middleton refers in *Father Hubbard's Tales* as 'a nest of boys able to ravish a man' (77).[7] Although the Paul's company had first started performing in the 1570s, they had been closed down in 1590–1 following their involvement through John Lyly's plays in the Martin Marlprelate controversy (see Gurr, 1987: 130–1), after which no children's drama had been available publicly for a decade. When they reopened in 1599 they quickly regained their popularity, and very soon were attracting not only an audience but also up-and-coming dramatists such as Marston, Jonson and Chapman. Certainly Shakespeare's jibes against them in *Hamlet* (II. ii. 346–52) suggest that the Children were perceived as a serious rival attraction to the adult companies in the public playhouses on the Bankside south of the river.

Paul's boys performed in an indoor, candle-lit theatre located in the precinct of St Paul's cathedral. The theatre was originally a 'private house in the hands of the Master [of the Choristers] . . . within the liberty of the cathedral and thus outside normal legal jurisdiction' (Gair, 1982: 55), and the term 'private' is used to distinguish all indoor theatre spaces – such as the Blackfriars and the Phoenix – from outdoor 'public' playhouses such as the Globe and the Swan. By the time Middleton worked for the Paul's company, the 'house' had been renovated for use exclusively as a theatre, and an extremely intimate one, holding an audience of 'perhaps less than 200 people' (Gurr, 1987: 22), possibly even as few as 100, all of whom were seated. Performances began at 4 p.m. and continued until about 6 p.m.

The Paul's stage appears to have comprised a two-storey façade at the rear, with a central double door (which may at times have been hung with a curtain) flanked by two narrower doors, and an upper level extending the full width, which was used both as an acting area and to accommodate the musicians. The dimensions of the main stage are not known for certain (Gair calculates it as 17 feet wide × 10 feet deep: 5 × 3 m), but it was evidently too small to accommodate spectators on stools, as was the practice on the much larger stage at the Blackfriars (see chapter 6). By Middleton's time the main stage had been fitted with a trap.

The composition of the audience included many who came to St Paul's to do business (the central aisle of the cathedral – Duke Humphrey's Walk – was a popular meeting place), people from the local neighbourhood and the young lawyers from the nearby Inns of Court. In comparison with the broader social cross-section attracted to the public playhouses, the audience may be described as 'select'. The higher entrance price would certainly have narrowed the social range of those who attended, and the fact that they performed on only one day each week (as opposed to the daily performances of the open-air playhouses) would have given the theatre the added cachet of exclusivity.

Topical satirical plays were a particularly popular element of the Paul's repertoire. Immediately prior to the presentation of *The Phoenix* the company had been involved in a scandal over *The Old Joiner of Aldgate*, a play (now lost) by George Chapman that dramatised very closely the sexual and business affairs of certain local inhabitants. The theatre may have seemed to be 'taking on the character of a tabloid newspaper' (Gair, 1982: 171), and the high moral tone of *The Phoenix* was perhaps in part an attempt to restore the respectability of the Paul's Boys' public profile.

We know very little of how Elizabethan and Jacobean adult

actors actually performed, and it is even more difficult for us to reconstruct the boys' performances in our imaginations. It seems likely that when they started playing, a main attraction lay in seeing children represent adults, and Brian Gibbons (1980: 67) has argued that the disparity between the boys' ages and the roles they played would have created a certain 'detachment' particularly suited to the satirical comedy in which they excelled. It seems likely that there must have been at least an element of parody and caricature in their performance, though Gair points out that they avoided false beards and moustaches, which implies that they eschewed unnecessary burlesque. Their song-school origins suggest that their singing would have been of very high quality (hence the particular importance and extensive use of music in the private theatres), and the texts of many of their plays, though they do not demand the same emotional range as those performed by the adult actors, indicate the boys' considerable ability in handling complex verse and prose.

Under Middleton's influence, however, the plays at Paul's became increasingly less specifically boys' plays, until virtually nothing remained to distinguish them from adult company material. One reason for this may have been that the boys were getting older: in 1606, when the Paul's company performed at Greenwich for King James and his brother-in-law, Christian IV of Denmark, a document refers to them as 'the Youthes of Paules', suggesting perhaps that they could no longer be properly described as 'Children'. As Gair notes, 'if the early teenagers of about fourteen who took the major parts in 1599 were still with the company in 1606, they would be over twenty by now' (1982: 154).

VI

*The Phoenix* is one of a number of 'disguised ruler' or 'absent monarch' plays (such as Marston's *The Malcontent* and *The Fawn*, Shakespeare's *Measure for Measure* and, at least superficially, Dekker and Webster's *Westward Ho!*) that appeared around 1604 in the indoor theatres and outdoor playhouses. All are concerned with questions of royal authority, and coincide with a considerable output of non-dramatic works on the same subject – a level of interest apparently stimulated by the accession of the new king.

*The Phoenix* opens with the Duke of Ferrara near death. Proditor, a treacherous noble, advises the Duke to send his son, Phoenix, to travel abroad, so leaving the coast clear for Proditor's own machinations. The prince decides to stay, however, and travelling in disguise around his kingdom in the company of his friend Fidelio, uncovers corruption at all levels of society, particularly marriages made for money and the dealings of dishonest lawyers. As in *Measure for Measure*, the presence of the true prince throughout the play reassures the audience that ultimately everything will be all right, and indeed, Phoenix eventually returns to the court, reveals himself and unmasks all the sinners, with each being treated in terms of a sickness to be cured. He banishes the traitor Proditor, punishes the other malefactors (there is none of the deliberate ambiguity of Shakespeare's ending in Middleton's play), and takes over the reins of government from his father, who willingly abdicates since now 'I know thee wise, canst both obey and reign' (V. i. 184).

It is regrettable that the only modern edition of *The Phoenix* is currently out of print, since the play offers an excellent starting point for a study of Middleton's dramatic work.[8] Middleton is a particularly self-repetitive writer, and the issues at the centre of *The Phoenix* – the use and abuse of power, the links between economic and sexual corruption – appear consistently throughout his work, while the skilful management of a number of plot-lines and the framework of irony in language and situation are elements that remain as hallmarks of his style.

The same is true of many of the dramatic and theatrical means by which Middleton expresses his ideas. For example, the play has close affinities with the secular Morality, seen in the allegorical naming of the characters – Fidelio (faithful), Falso (false), Proditor (Treacherous), and so on – and in the pattern of *exemplum* (action) followed by *interpretation*, usually in the form of a speech by Phoenix directly addressed to the audience, in which he comments on the corruption of a particular institution or moral principle. Such an approach is consistent with Middleton's didactic impulse, and is an aspect of his dramatic technique that – in various formations – recurs throughout his plays, pageants and masques.[9]

In addition to this blend of 'allegorical' elements with the 'realistic' satirical treatment of characters and events, Middleton displays his ability to create scenes that carry great symbolic weight: where the action of the scene embodies its meaning. A startling (if difficult) example in this play is II. iii. It takes the form of a practice fencing match between Tangle and Falso, two corrupt lawyers, in which Tangle's 'Rapier is my attorney, and my Dagger his clerk' (203–4). Various weapons are identified with law terms ('Your longsword, that's a writ of delay' – 166) and fencing set-pieces with legal manoeuvres ('Now follows a writ of execution; a *capias utlagatum* gives you a wound mortal, trips up your heels, and lays you i' th' counter. [Overthrows him]' – 250–2).

The scene provides an early example of Middleton's use of 'game' and 'earnest'. The 'game' (the fencing match) is an active, tangible metaphor for the 'earnest' (the cut and thrust of the legal world) that exists in the audience's reality. It prefigures Middleton's frequent use of this traditional dramatic device, seen in his presentation of actual games (such as those played by the Ward and Sordido and the celebrated chess game in *Women Beware Women*), the play/masque-within-a-play (in, among others, *Women Beware Women*, *A Mad World, My Masters*, *Hengist, King of Kent* and *The Second Maiden's Tragedy*), and, most extensively, the entire structure of *A Game at Chess*.

The play's conclusion, in which order is restored, may have reminded the audience that King James had a promising young son in Prince Henry (Heinemann, 1982: 72). However, it seems rather early in James's reign to be casting him, even by the most tangential implication, as the dying old Duke, especially in a play that, as the title-page informs us, was performed for him and in which Middleton might be aiming to praise and please his king. Since the Phoenix was a symbol frequently associated with King James (Thomas Dekker had employed it in his contribution to James's royal entry into London in 1604), it is more likely that the play cast James in that role in order to demonstrate that he was the legitimate and true heir of Elizabeth I.

Rather than attempting to make specific identifications, how-

ever, it is more important to note that at this stage of his career
Middleton evidently considered it possible to represent an 'ideal
ruler' who would be able to restore the realm to good health,
and to place such an authority figure unambiguously at the
centre of his play. The result, dramatically, is that moral lessons
are imposed from one character on the others (and, by implication, on the audience), and are stated rather than woven into
the fabric of the play, making it overtly didactic in tone and
style. Middleton never lost his impulse to scourge and attack
public and personal vice, but he did develop a style of writing
that let his criticism emerge from the interaction of characters
and events, so implicating and involving the audience, rather
than preaching to them.

## VII

By the time he finished *The Phoenix* Middleton had engaged, in
his early poetry, prose and plays, with areas of subject-matter,
aspects of dramatic form and theatrical strategies that he would
explore, develop and experiment with in the comedies, tragicomedies and tragedies of his remaining career. *The Phoenix*
demonstrates many characteristics of the then-burgeoning genre
of city comedy, and it was in the brilliant series of such
comedies that he wrote in the next few years for the boys'
companies that Middleton found increasingly his own,
individual voice, and established his reputation as a playwright.

# 2
# City Comedies:
## 'Michaelmas Term',
## 'A Mad World, My Masters',
## 'A Trick to Catch the Old One'

City comedy, as Alexander Leggatt (1973: 3) has written, 'is one of those conveniently vague terms that seem serviceable enough until an attempt is made to define them'. It is possible, however, to identify some of the main characteristics of this genre, which enjoyed enormous popularity during the first decade of the seventeenth century, above all through the comedies of Ben Jonson (whom Gibbons describes as the genre's 'founder' – 1980: 5), John Marston and Middleton himself.[1]

The form of these comedies is a blend of new, experimental dramatic techniques and earlier forms of drama such as the Morality play and the Roman intrigue comedy of Plautus and Terence. In addition, they show the influence of contemporary non-dramatic literature, mainly satire, complaint, and prose pamphlets describing the London underworld (see Rowe, 1979; Gibbons, 1980, Peter, 1956). The content of the plays was informed by current social issues, as the playwrights sought to 'dramatize the complex process of conducting economic and social relations in a newly forming urban environment' (Rose, 1988: 43). As many critics have observed, the plays do not offer what might be termed an 'economic analysis' of the period, but they do provide an acerbic depiction of it, and frequently prefigure collisions and tensions that were to become acute in English society as the century progressed.[2]

The setting of the plays is usually London, and even when a large part of the action takes place elsewhere (as in *A Mad World, My Masters*, for example, much of which is set in Bedfordshire) it is the attitudes to life prevalent in the city that predominate, and which are thrown into greater relief by their contrast with the attitudes of the country. This comparison of city corruption with rural straightforwardness that is so prevalent in Jacobean drama had slowly emerged during the sixteenth century. The 'city' had become a dramatic metaphor, increasingly associated with crime, acquisitiveness and sexual immorality (Tydeman, 1985). As the campaigning pamphleteer Robert Crowley wrote of London in 1550:

> And this is a City
> In name, but, in deed,
> It is a pack of people
> That seek after meed;
> For officers and all
> Do seek their own gain,
> But for the wealth of the commons
> No one taketh pain.
> An hell without order,
> I may well it call,
> When every man is for himself,
> And no man for all.
> (from *One and thyrtye Epigrammes*)

Crowley's general equation – that city equals greed and self-interest – was honed to an even sharper edge by the very rapid growth of London during this period as rich and poor in their thousands flooded into the capital, with all the acute social pressures which that expansion brought. Although figures vary, it seems that the population of London increased from around 50,000 in Henry VIII's reign to 160–180,000 in 1600, with a further rise by 1640. It helps to put these figures in context if one remembers that the second largest city in England at this time was Norwich with a population of 20–30,000, and that only

Birmingham, Bristol, Exeter, Newcastle and York had more than 10,000 inhabitants: as King James himself observed: 'all the country is gotten into London: so as with time England will only be London, and the whole country be left waste'.

London's growth was due to its position as the centre of virtually everything. It was the seat of government, the main residence of the court, the only banking centre, the centre of publishing, and the home of most government officials and professional people. It controlled three-quarters of England's foreign trade and dominated domestic markets. It had the largest concentration of industrial workers anywhere in the country, many of them working in industries that were to be found only in London.[3]

In these circumstances, and this environment, crime and business could both expect to flourish. Pre-eminent amongst the criminal classes were 'cony-catchers' (literally rabbit catchers), swindlers and con-men whose activities were recorded in minute, if somewhat embellished, detail by Robert Greene, who, in the early 1590s, produced a series of pamphlets in which he set out 'those pernicious sleights that hath brought many ignorant men to confusion'. Similarities abound between the characters and events described in this cony-catching literature and represented in the city comedies: the commodities swindles Greene (himself a playwright) dramatically portrays in his *Notable Discovery of Cozenage* (1591), for example, are identical to those that form the basis of the gulling of Richard Easy in *Michaelmas Term*, and II. iii of *Your Five Gallants* (c. 1604–7; another of Middleton's early comedies), set in the Mitre inn, is a brilliant scene of deceit and trickery that could come straight from one of the pamphlets.

In 1592, a reply to Greene was published under the pseudonym of Cuthbert Conycatcher (possibly Greene himself taking a characteristically provocative stance). In this pamphlet – *The Defence of Cony Catching, or, A Confutation of those two injurious pamphlets published by R.G. against the practitioners of many Nimble-witted and mystical sciences* – 'Cuthbert' points out the similarities between the con-man and the apparently respectable merchant/usurer:

You decipher poor cony-catchers, that perhaps with a trick at cards win forty shillings from a churl that can spare it, and never talk of these caterpillars that undo the poor, ruin whole lordships, infect the commonwealth, and delight in nothing but in wrongful extorting and purloining of pelf, when as such be the greatest cony catchers of all . . . these fox-furred gentlemen that hide under their gowns faced with foins [marten's fur] more falsehood than all the cony catchers in England beside, those miserable usurers, I mean.[4]

It is a perspective shared by Middleton, who shows the tricks of the swindlers being practised by lawyers and merchants. Indeed, merchants were becoming very wealthy indeed, the richest of them wealthier than most peers. They could afford to lend money to the king, to the nobility (much of this money being used to finance the extravagances and corruption of life at court, both common targets of dramatists), and to country aristocracy down on their luck. In return they gained not just money from the high interest often charged, but power and, not infrequently, land (Gibbons, 1980: 27–33).

As the hub of the social and political world in England, London attracted great numbers of the rural aristocracy and gentry, and this period sees the beginning of the London 'season'. Some came (often accompanied by their wives and children) to enjoy the leisure industries thrown up by the city's wealth and expansion, others to seek patronage and advancement at court, while large numbers came to undertake legal action. Some came to try to raise money through investment in various business enterprises or in a foreign expedition, by borrowing, by making an advantageous marriage for themselves or their children, or by selling their land. Many, especially the young gentlemen fresh from the country, seduced by the pleasures of the city but surprised at the cost, became easy prey for unscrupulous con-men.

The rise in commercial strength of the London merchant coincided with an economic crisis for the land-owning gentry, often forced to mortgage their estates to maintain them or, like the foolish young heir in the Ant's 'Ploughman' tale, to sell them completely, along with their tenants, to pay for their new city life-style. Unable to repay the mortgage, and perhaps without the 'wit' of a Witgood to regain it through other methods, the land was lost to the money-lender (who might be a merchant or lawyer) who thereby gained the social status that land in the country could add to wealth.

Ben Jonson described the process in *The Devil Is An Ass*:

> We see those changes daily: the fair lands
> That were the client's, are the lawyer's now;
> And those rich manors there, of goodman tailor's,
> Had once more wood upon 'em than the yard
> By which th'were measur'd out of the last purchase.
> Nature hath these vicissitudes. She makes
> No man a state of perpetuity, sir.
>
> (II. iv. 33–9)

Jonson was right to identify Jacobean society as not being in a 'state of perpetuity'. It was, in fact, a society in a state of flux, changing its social structure from one based on inherited status and wealth (both often bound up in land) to one based on capital, with unprecedented social mobility, vertically and horizontally. It was not an entirely new phenomenon; like so many aspects of Jacobean life its origins can be found in Elizabeth's reign. In his survey of England in 1577, William Harrison had already observed shifts in the traditional social hierarchy:

> In this place also are our merchants to be installed, as amongst the citizens (although they often change estate with gentlemen, as gentlemen do with them, by mutual conversion of the one into the other) whose number is increased in these days.

During the early years of the seventeenth century, however, the problem became increasingly acute, bringing with it a growing sense of both opportunity and insecurity. In these circumstances, the inevitable conflicts between the merchants and the gentry, the lawyers and their clients, the citizen and the courtier, became the subject-matter – and these figures the characters – of much of the drama.

Alexander Leggatt defines 'city' comedies as plays about citizens, though not necessarily written for them, or supporting their attitudes and values. Although there are exceptions

(Dekker and Webster's derivative *Westward Ho!*, for example), the satirical comedies written for the boys' companies tend to take the gentry's side against the citizen, whereas the opposite is true of those plays like Dekker's *The Shoemakers' Holiday* or Heywood's *The Fair Maid of the West*, which were presented in the open-air playhouses by adult companies and which tended to offer moral lessons and to celebrate rather than criticise London and its merchants (Leggatt, 1973: 10). It is noticeable, however, that Middleton's plays at this stage of his career seem to be equally critical of anti-social or stupid behaviour on the part of either gentleman or citizen. Nor does Middleton make blanket condemnations. He does not attack lawyers or merchants in general, but specifically those who are corrupt in their dealings. In *Michaelmas Term*, for example, it is a member of Quomodo's own guild – the Drapers' Company – who points out the devious means by which Quomodo has become rich:

LIVERYMAN:  Who, Quomodo? Merely enriched by shifts
And coz'nages, believe it.  (IV. iv. 16–17)

The basic structure of Middleton's city comedies is the intrigue plot, the complexity of which exemplifies the acts of deception in the world outside the theatre that the play mirrors, rather than being a display of ingeniously clever plotting for its own sake. It is as if (in the established tradition of the Morality play) the audience's enjoyment of the play activity, or the seductiveness of the delight in its action, is intended to place them in the same position as those characters who are equally seduced by pleasure and cleverness within the play itself. The theme of deception also accounts for the wide variety of uses of 'disguise' in the plays, and for the extensive use of self-reflexive elements (commonly associated with boys' companies) such as the play-within-a-play and 'role' playing. In addition, city comedies frequently draw on specific events and personalities that the audience could identify and thereby recognise the underlying truth of the action, even if its actual mode of presentation was heightened for satiric purposes.

The comedies he wrote for the boys' companies are sometimes discussed in terms of Middleton's 'development' as a writer. Leaving aside the question of whether such an approach is critically desirable (is *A Trick to Catch the Old One* a 'better' play than *Michaelmas Term* because of its different organisation of material?), it should be remembered that, on present knowledge, the dating of these plays simply does not allow such an approach to be valid. It is more advisable, therefore, to consider each play on its own terms, within the context of city comedy as a genre.

Within the (rather loose) framework of the genre, Middleton constantly explores the relationship between the content of the plays and the form in which the ideas are dramatised, as well as the various combinations of tone and mood such stylistic collisions might produce – a range of experiment that will become clear from an analysis of three representative plays from the period 1604–6.[5]

## 'MICHAELMAS TERM'

According to the title-page of the first edition published in 1607, the play had been 'sundry times acted by the Children of Paul's'. No author's name was given (nor was it in the second quarto of 1629–30), but the attribution to Middleton, first made in 1656, has never been seriously challenged. The play was probably written and performed sometime in 1605.

I

As was common practice at the indoor theatres, the play opens with a short Induction (a scene introducing the play and performance but separated from the actual story of the play), in which the personification of 'Michaelmas Term' symbolically exchanges a white robe ('that weed is for the country' – l. 2) for a black one, since:

> We must be civil now, and match our evil,
> Who first made civil black, he pleased the devil.
>                                (3–4)[6]

After Michaelmas Term has stressed the wealth he is about to
amass through the ensuing litigation, a short dumb-show to
music follows in which the other three law terms bring in a poor
man, dress him in fine clothes, and give him a page and a
pander. Michaelmas Term is addressed by the other three as the
'father of the Terms' and 'patron of our hopes', apt titles, since
coming after the summer vacation in which the courts did not
sit, Michaelmas Term was the busiest and most profitable time
for the lawyers:

3rd TERM:
  Many new fools come up and fee thee.
2nd TERM
  Let 'em pay dear enough that see thee.   (37–8)


After the Terms exit, Michaelmas Term addresses the audience, directly linking the world of the play with that of the
theatre: 'in cheaper terms I salute you; for ours have but
sixpenny fees [the minimum price of admission at Paul's] all the
year long, yet we despatch you in two hours without demur;
your suits hang not long here after candles be lighted [plays
began at about 4 p.m. and finished before 6 p.m. – comparable
to the 'two hours traffic of the stage' at the open-air playhouses,
though there performances started at 2 p.m.]' (64–6).
   The Induction serves a number of purposes: it establishes the
connection made throughout the play between underhand legal
deals and whoring, money and sex; it sets place and time, and
draws attention to the close association between 'costume' and
'role' that is a central theme of the play. By emphasising that
what follows is a *play*, a representation of events in the world
outside the theatre where those 'fools i'th'house' [i.e. the young
men in the audience] may be 'fondly deceived' just as Easy will
be, but in their case with very real, and serious results, the
Induction establishes that the play's issues are the personal
concern of many of its audience.

II

> Go, make my coarse commodities look sleek,
> With subtle art beguile the honest eye.
>
> (I. i. 81–2)

The central action of the play concerns the gulling of a naïve young heir from the country – Richard Easy – by the unscrupulous linen-draper Ephestian Quomodo and his 'spirits', Shortyard and Falselight. The presentation of Quomodo owes much to the traditional Vice figure, but the character may well be based more directly on a true-life merchant named Howe ('quomodo' is the Latin word for 'how'), who was convicted by the Court of Star Chamber on 18 June 1596 for a con-trick similar to that employed in the play:

> The first case was an information by the Queen's Attorney against one Howe, a broker, and Easte, a solicitor, for 'coseninge diuers yonge gentlemen', and procuring them to enter into bonds, statutes, recognizances and confessions of actions by attorney (which bound them although under age, and which could not be avoided when they came to full age).[7]

After the con-men had been sentenced, the Lord Treasurer wished 'those yt make the playes to make a Comedie hereof, & to acte it wth these names', and though the gap in time between this judgement and the composition of Middleton's play suggests that *Michaelmas Term* was not written in direct response to the Lord Treasurer's request, it is by no means impossible that the case and its protagonists provided a source. It is also possible that a more recent figure called Howe, whose affairs had been dramatised by George Chapman in a scandal-making play, *The Old Joiner of Aldgate*, performed only a short time before at Paul's and which Middleton certainly knew (see chapter 1), gave him the idea for the name. But there is no real need to identify a particular individual since actual incidents of swindles such as one finds in this and other of Middleton's comedies are frequently recorded. R. C. Bald quotes the case of Woodleef *v.* Frizer (the same Ingram Frizer who was involved in the death of Christopher Marlowe):

Widow Anne Woodleef of Aylesbury, Bucks., and her son,
Drew, accuse Ingram Frizer of practising, with the aid of
Nicholas Skeres, a series of frauds on the said Drew, under
pretence of lending him ready money. Frizer's first device
was to get a signed bond for £60 from Drew, against an
assurance that he would lend Drew a similar amount in cash.
When it came to the point, Frizer pretended that he had no
ready money, and offered Drew instead some cannon, or
great iron pieces, which he had on Tower Hill. These Drew
was forced to accept; but he begged Frizer to sell them for
him. Frizer made as though to sell them, and returned shortly
after with £30 as the proceeds. Drew accuses him of never
offering the guns for sale, and of swindling him out of the
other £30.[8]

The con-trick played on Richard Easy is more complex than this,
but the sequence of events is very similar and underlines the
fact that the audience would instantly recognise the activities of
the crooks in the play as true to life. Their knowledge of such
cases would have reminded the audience that Richard Easy's
experience was not unique, and that being taken in by clever
professionals like Quomodo and his cronies was not necessarily
a sign of total stupidity. As Michaelmas Term says in the
Induction, the play will not present 'any great quarrels in law',
but merely 'those familiar accidents, which happened in town in
the circumference of those six weeks whereof Michaelmas Term
is lord' (70–3), a claim for documentary realism in respect of the
play's subject matter that is unlikely to have been challenged.


### III

Oh, my most cheerful spirit, go, dispatch!
Gentry is the chief fish we tradesmen catch.
(I. i. 131–2)

Quomodo has been busy during the summer months preceding
Michaelmas Term. In Essex he has seen the lands of the young
heir, Richard Easy, and means to secure them for himself. Seeing

that Easy has arrived in the city, Quomodo sets one of his 'spirits' to:

> Keep foot by foot with him, out-dare his expenses,
> Flatter, dice, and brothel to him;
> Give him a sweet taste of sensuality;
> Train him to every wasteful sin, that he
> May quickly need health, but especially money;
> (I. i. 120–4)

From their first acquaintance with Easy in II. i, through to the final surrender of his land in IV. i, the 'hoist' is set out in careful detail, and the central scene, where the 'sting' is enacted (II. iii), is rightly described by Richard Levin as 'Middleton's most brilliant achievement in this genre, worthy to be compared to any of the more famous "gulling" scenes in Jonson's major comedies' (Levin, 1966: xiv). The con-trick is so clever, its execution so skilful (it has been suggested that an apt subtitle for the play would be *A Trick to Catch the Young One*), that a certain amount of the audience's pleasure undoubtedly lies in watching it carried out. This has led some critics of the play to question whether the enjoyment Quomodo provides does not adversely affect Middleton's ability to criticise and punish him. R. B. Parker writes that: 'uneasiness of tone and incredible retribution can be seen in all Middleton's early comedies, caused in each case by his difficulty in bringing immoral comic characters to severe condemnation' (Parker, 1960: 183). Ruby Chatterji shares this view, and finds that the 'cony-catching interest of the beginning and the retributive justice of the end are evidently at variance' (Chatterji, 1968: 359). Although it may be true that in *A Trick to Catch the Old One* Middleton is more successful in implying, rather than stating, moral censure, criticism of Quomodo is sustained throughout the play, and is not confined to the last scene.

Middleton constantly stresses the violence and cruelty of Quomodo's actions. In I. i, when he first describes the lands he has seen, Quomodo speaks of his wish to 'cleave the air in twain [with the pun on 'heir'] . . . to murder his estate,/Stifle his right in some detested prison' and of the 'deadly enmity' that exists between the gentry and merchant/citizens like himself. In the

three scenes in which Easy is destroyed (II. iii, III. iv and IV. i),
Quomodo's wife Thomasine observes and comments on the
action. In the first two she watches from the upper level, acting
as a commentator to mediate the action on the main stage and
guide our response. This is an early example of Middleton's use
of the physical structure of the stage to provide the audience
simultaneously with a double perspective, the brilliant apo-
theosis of which is achieved in the chess game/rape in *Women
Beware Women*. Consequently, while on one level we perceive the
scene as the enjoyable gulling of a none-too-wise young man
from the country, Thomasine makes us perceive it also as an
execution at which the victim, so eager is he to participate, helps
in his own disembowelling. She sees herself (and, by implication, makes us see ourselves) as the heartless spectators at the
event:

> Why stand I here (as late our graceless dames
> That found no eyes) to see that gentleman
> Alive in state and credit, executed,
> Help to rip up himself, does all he can?
> 			(II. iii. 202–5)

Her lines 'Why am I wife to him that is no man/I suffer in that
gentleman's confusion' (207–8) must at least call in question our
own relationship with Quomodo and attitude to his actions. It is
worth noting here the added resonance the lines may have had
for the original Paul's audience: the churchyard was a site where
executions took place, one of the most celebrated being that of
Henry Garnet on 3 May 1606 for his part in the Gunpowder
Plot, which was 'transacted, not in secret hugger-mugger, but
openly, and as it were upon the Stage'.[9]
   The asides as Easy finally signs the bond – repeated images of
severing and cutting interposed with the image of Christmas
comfort – underline the violence of what we have witnessed.
Thomasine again interprets the scene:

QUOMODO:
   Now I begin to set one foot upon the land. Methinks I am

felling of trees already; we shall have some Essex logs yet
to keep Christmas with, and that's a comfort.
THOMASINE:
Now is he quart'ring out; the executioner
Strides over him; with his own blood he writes.
I am no dame that can endure such sights. *Exit*
SHORTYARD:
So his right wing is cut; he will not fly far
Past the two city hazards, Poultry and Wood Street.
(338–45)

A similar effect is achieved in III. iv, where Thomasine once
more observes the action. Presumably she is present from the
start of the scene, as it is important that she should see
Quomodo in full-flight and overhear his soliloquies if her
actions in support of Easy are to be seen to be motivated by a
realisation and rejection of her husband's nature, and not only
by sexual desire. Middleton makes clear, however, that Thomasine's frustration is caused by Quomodo's apparent neglect of
sexual activity in favour of the physical and emotional satisfaction he gains from land ('They're busy 'bout our wives, we
'bout their lands' – I. i. 107), which Quomodo describes as if
referring to a woman:

Oh, that sweet, neat, comely, proper, delicate parcel of land,
like a fine gentlewoman i'th' waist, not so great as pretty,
pretty  (II. iii. 82–5).

The mediating effect is achieved by Thomasine's single
interjection ('The more I grieve' – 148) towards the middle of the
scene as Easy seeks despairingly for those who will save him
from Quomodo, and by her comment at the end of the scene in
which she forcefully identifies both the desperateness of Easy's
position, and the jealousy and violence of Quomodo:

                thy misery but begins;
'To beguile goodness is the core of sins.'
My love is such unto thee, that I die
As often as thou drinkst up injury,
Yet have no means to warn thee from't; for 'he

That sows in craft does rape in jealousy.'
                                                (242–7)

In these ways, Middleton ensures that our critical awareness
of Quomodo is kept active at times when we, too, might be
deceived by him and his spirits, and so sustains a darker side to
the play that underlines the basic savagery of the society and
creates in the audience a balance between engagement and
detachment. It is a mixture of comic and serious angles of vision,
presented simultaneously, that is characteristic of Middleton
(and much of the thought of his time), and an early example of
that particular blend of contrasting tones and moods that is a
hallmark of his style.


                                 IV


This central plot of the deception of Richard Easy is interwoven
with two further, separate plots that support and develop the
governing ideas of the play. In one, the unattractive and
unscrupulous Andrew Gruel (who has, with unconscious irony,
changed his name to Lethe)[10] tries to gain Quomodo's daughter
Susan in marriage, while still maintaining a Country Wench
procured for him by his pander, Hellgill. His rival for Susan's
hand is a young gallant, Rearage, who (like his friend Salewood)
wastes away his inheritance on the high-life in London. Susan's
mother, Thomasine, favours Rearage, while Quomodo prefers
the socially upward-thrusting Lethe:

QUOMODO:
    Pray, what's Master Rearage whom you plead for so?
THOMASINE:
    Why, first, he is a gentleman.
QUOMODO:
    Ay, he's often first a gentleman that's last a beggar

    .  .  .  .  .  .  .  .  .  .  .  .  .  .  .  .  .  .  .  .
    Thou know'st, beside, we undo gentlemen daily.
THOMASINE:
    That makes so few of 'em marry with our daughters,
    unless it be one green fool or other. Next, Master Rearage

has land and living, tother but his walk i'th' street, and his
snatching diet; he's able to entertain you in a fair house of
his own, tother in some nook or corner, or place us behind
the cloth like a company of puppets; at his house you shall
be served curiously, sit down and eat your meat with
leisure; there we must be glad to take it standing, and
without either salt, cloth, or trencher, and say we are
befriended too. (II. iii. 48–64)

This traditional view of the distinction between 'New Men'
and the landed gentry may be another reason why Thomasine is
inclined to side with Easy against her husband, while the
similarities between Quomodo and Lethe further explain why
the draper wishes to have Lethe for his son-in-law. Just as Lethe
and Quomodo are linked (both, too, being defeated by gentlemen), Lethe is involved in the third plot, which concerns the fate
in London of the Country Wench. Throughout the play, in
language, action and imagery, connections are made between
sex and money, and the procuring of the girl for Lethe by the
appropriately named Hellgill parallels the procuring of Easy's
land (he is, of course, a Country Gentleman) by Shortyard and
Falselight. It puts into action, as it were, Quomodo's analogy of
land and a woman's body. The Wench is not a very fully
developed character, but it is interesting to see that even in her
case Middleton insists that the force of economics in human
affairs cannot be ignored – especially in the market-place of sex.
And it is important to note that, even if he does not excuse her
actions (she seems unable to resist the temptation of fine gowns
and jewels that open the door to her prostitution, for example),
he gives at least some reason for her behaviour and so tempers
any rush to judgement on the part of the audience (IV. ii).

## V

This is the fruit of craft:
Like him that shoots up high, looks for the shaft,
And finds it in his forehead, so does hit
The arrow of our fate: wit destroys wit.
(V. i. 41–4)

The pinnacle of Quomodo's success in the play comes in IV. i, when he finally gets hold of Easy's land. The moment is charged with Quomodo's smug ruthlessness, and Easy's and Thomasine's condemnation of him:

QUOMODO:
> Why, Thomasine, Master Easy is come from Essex; bid him welcome in a cup of small beer.

THOMASINE:
> [*Aside*] Not only vild [vile], but in it tyrannous.

QUOMODO:
> If it please you, sir, you know the house; you may visit us often, and dine with us once a quarter.

EASY:
> Confusion light on you, your wealth, and heir;
> Worm gnaw your conscience, as the moth your ware!
> I am not the first heir that rob'd or beg'd.

> (51–8)

The curse is not long in coming true. At this moment of triumph, Quomodo overreaches himself, interrupting his fantasy of deforestation and holiday jaunts down to his new country estate with a thought of a 'toy', a trick. He decides to feign his own death, and in a disguise of his own:

> note the condition of all: how pitiful my wife takes my death . . . my daughter's marrying to my will and liking; and my son's affection after my disposing; for, to conclude, I am as jealous of this land as of my wife, to know what would become of it after my decease. (IV. i. 104–112)

Until this moment, although deceitful, Quomodo has left the taking of physical disguise to his henchmen, while he has been the 'author' of the play, guiding its events and controlling the other characters. Now, in effect, he writes himself out, marginalises himself, and events cease to go as he wishes: no one mourns him with any genuine feeling (Middleton's stage direction notes that the funeral is 'a counterfeit corse . . . [with] all the mourners equally counterfeit' – IV. iv. 51).

Quomodo's self-confidence blinds him to the truth, and much

of the comedy of the last act derives from the irony of Quomodo's misinterpretation of others' actions. Thomasine marries Easy and tricks Quomodo into relinquishing any further claims in her or the house; his son Sim is easily and immediately tricked out of his inheritance by Shortyard; his daughter Susan chooses to marry Rearage rather than Lethe; and Quomodo himself is brought before a judge where he is forced to admit to his true identity and his true nature.

This 'trial scene' allows Middleton to impose judgement on Quomodo, but the climax develops from the draper's over-confidence matched against the united efforts of Thomasine and Easy, both of whom are empowered by Quomodo's self-inflicted absence from centre stage. Easy may be gullible, but he is neither culpable nor irredeemably stupid, and the ease with which now Quomodo himself is deceived by the play-acting of others (Thomasine's affected grief at his 'funeral', for example) underlines this. In IV. iii, Shortyard emphasises that in Easy's case:

> Only good confidence did make him foolish,
> And not the lack of sense, that was not it;
> 'Tis worldly craft beats down a scholar's wit.
>                               (15–7)

and Easy's behaviour and language in the last act support this view. Consequently, Easy's revival and the draper's fall do not rely on unacceptable shifts in the personalities of the central characters, but develop from the interaction of those characters and the events that have gone before.

The closing moments of the play are concerned with tying up loose ends – having been 'seiz'd in shame' (V. iii. 98) with the Country Wench on his wedding morning, Lethe is ordered to marry her and sentenced to be whipped; Mother Gruel has her son's identity revealed to her and publicly rebukes him; Quomodo banishes Shortyard; and, in order to round things off and so that 'all error from our works may stand' (167), the Judge banishes Falselight.

If this were all, the play would appear to have moved to a conventional close, righted all wrongs and punished all wrongdoers. But the ending of the play has a sour taste, since it appears from the text that although the Judge upholds the return of Easy's lands and Quomodo's loss of money, he does not uphold the marriage of Thomasine and Easy. Despite the fact that they have married and presumably consummated their relationship, the Judge returns the unwilling woman to her original husband. In this way, Middleton denies the play a sense of complete 'closure', and sustains in the audience a level of questioning and 'distance'. Although the 'moral' is expounded and retribution allotted, it is a woman who finds herself powerless, and who is treated in the same way as the money and the lands: that is, as the property of men. It is true that Middleton's earliest work, such as his teenage poem *The Wisdom of Solomon Paraphrased*, demonstrated a conventional misogyny, but these early comedies show this attitude shifting as the interest in and complex portrayal of women for which Middleton is known begins to emerge, and as the position of women in domestic and social life moves increasingly to the centre of his concerns.

## 'A MAD WORLD, MY MASTERS'

*A Mad World* was entered in the Stationer's Register and printed in 1608, and according to the title-page the printed text is 'As it hath bin lately in Action by the Children of Paules'. Composition has been dated sometime between July 1605 and July 1606 when it appears the Paul's company ceased playing on a regular basis.

### I

In *Michaelmas Term* 'disguise', 'apparel' and 'role playing' are not simply devices employed to set up and further the intrigue (as they are in *The Phoenix*), but have a symbolic function that underscores the play's treatment of deception. In *A Mad World* these devices are carried still further. The whole play is suffused with the terminology of acting, culminating in a 'play within a play' in which 'illusion' and 'reality' are enmeshed.

The play as a whole maintains the basic framework of the city comedy – a complicated intrigue plot with a number of intriguers striving for supremacy – and the typical characters and themes of the genre – youth versus age, close links between lust for money and lust for sex, and so on. There are differences from *Michaelmas Term*, however. Much of the action is removed out of London, and the play is not as dense with topical and topographical references. Nor is the central conflict here between class enemies, but between members of the same family; although Sir Bounteous is the target of his grandson, Richard Follywit's, intrigues, they are not embittered adversaries, and the tone of the play is consequently less sharp.

Sir Bounteous (Follywit and he both tell us) has every intention of leaving his money to his grandson when he dies, and they appear basically fond of each other. Follywit speaks of his 'frolic grandsire' (I. i. 40) and Sir Bounteous is quick to defend his grandson to Lord Owemuch (who is, in fact, Follywit in disguise):

> SIR BOUNTEOUS: I have a grandchild, my lord. I love him, and when I die I'll do somewhat for him. . . . Some comic pranks he has been guilty of, but I'll pawn my credit for him, an honest, trusty, bosom.
> FOLLYWIT: And that's worth all, sir.
> SIR BOUNTEOUS: And that's worth all indeed, my lord, for he's like to have all when I die.
>
> (II. i. 117–26)[11]

In his other city comedies Middleton attacks specific targets – such as spendthrift gallants, foolish country heirs, merchant-usurers and so on – and through their interaction illuminates particular social conflicts and the rottenness of lives driven by greed. In this play, however, he explores two major themes that are frequently reworked in later plays: the constraining roles women are forced by men to play, and secondly, deception – of others, and, even more dangerous, of oneself. Middleton examines what happens when a personality becomes so obsessive – Follywit with his endless intrigues, Sir Bounteous with his hospitality, Harebrain's jealousy or Brothel's sexual passion – that judgement is blinded. The play, in its component parts and its overall effect, explores the deception of the senses resulting from reason being distorted by passion – in essence, the same theme of which Middleton (with Rowley) explored the tragic consequences in *The Changeling*.

The sequence of Follywit's intrigues to trick his irrepressible uncle provides one of Middleton's most cleverly structured and serpentine plots, and it is perfectly possible to enjoy the play simply on the level of the intrigue (as, for example, R. H. Barker does, considering it no more than a light-hearted comedy). Brilliantly constructed and funny as it is, however, the play operates on a much more complex series of levels than this view suggests, as Middleton presents a number of scenes in which he explores the idea that what we see and hear and consequently conceive to be the 'truth' may not be what it seems.

## II

The first meeting of Sir Bounteous and (the disguised) Follywit (II. i) is concluded with an entertainment:

> SIR BOUNTEOUS:  My organist!
> *The organs play, and cover'd dishes march over the stage*
> Come, my lord, how does your honour relish my organ?
> FOLLYWIT:  A very proud air, i'faith, sir.
> SIR BOUNTEOUS:  Oh, how can't choose? A Walloon plays upon 'em, and a Welshman blows wind in their breech. *Exeunt.*
> *A song to the organs*
>
> (151–5)

The song or music with which it was customary to divide the acts of the play in the private theatres exists in the time and space of the play and of the audience, and a song is obviously appropriate for a song-school company. But Middleton has gone further than this by 'making a feature of a novel instrument at Paul's, the regals or portable organ' (Gair, 1982: 154), and so establishing the interpenetration of the actual space of the auditorium and the fictional space of Sir Bounteous's hall. There are other similar devices. In II. ii there is a reference to 'the curtains . . . wrought in Venice, with the story of the prodigal child in silk and gold' (l. 6). On one level this is an ironical comment made unwittingly by Sir Bounteous to his prodigal grandson, but it may also refer to the 'painted cloths' known to have hung in theatres and often inscribed with elevating mottos. Such a cloth depicting the story of the prodigal son may have hung in the theatre (perhaps across the rear of the stage as in the illustration on the title-page of Nathaniel Richards's play, *Messalina*), providing an appropriately ironic visual emblem/background to the action.

The play at all levels is alert to its own nature as a play, and to the conscious roles adopted, and performances given, by its leading characters. Throughout, Follywit and others take on different roles, and the play stresses how easily this can be done. A Lord can be simulated with 'A French ruff, a thin beard, and a strong perfume', with a small cast of extras in 'blue coats' (I. i. 72–3) to add the final touch of verisimilitude; a prostitute may even impersonate a virgin simply by displaying 'a politic conveyance,/A sincere carriage, a religious eyebrow' (I. i. 160–1).

Enforcing the links between the stage and audience worlds engages the audience directly in the events and attitudes of the play, and the emphasis on theatrical and social role-playing provides a metaphor for Middleton's examination of the conventional view of women. Although the use of the 'world as stage' metaphor was a commonplace in the drama of the period, and plays written for the boys' companies are particularly noted for their self-conscious theatricality, Middleton is here employing these self-reflexive elements to particular ends and not merely following a theatrical vogue.

## III

The play's other plot-line concerns the attempt by Penitent Brothel to seduce the not-unwilling wife of the pathologically jealous Master Harebrain, aided by the Courtesan, Frank Gullman. Harebrain, unaware of Frank's true profession, encourages her to instruct his wife in matters of morality. He displays the distorted morality so often attacked by Middleton, since although he decries the sin of adultery, he is quick to justify usury, bribery and sloth. His attempt to control his wife is what rebounds on him. As Simon Shepherd neatly puts it:

> Since Harebrain is one of those males who constructs an image of what women are, who keeps women separate but filters bits of them through into a world that is his, he is punished by his creations. (Shepherd, 1981: 64)

In this way, Middleton illustrates the affinities between Harebrain and Follywit. One is jealous, the other a roué: both are punished for failing to recognise the rights and independent existences of women.

Although the two plots are further linked at the level of character through Frank (who is also the mistress of Sir Bounteous and eventually becomes the wife of the unsuspecting Follywit), the relationship between them has been strongly criticised, generally on the grounds that one (Follywit/Sir Bounteous) maintains a light-hearted tone and is not much troubled with morality, whereas the Penitent plot is used (not very successfully, some critics argue) to carry the more serious moral tone of the play.

Within this general criticism, the sudden conversion of Penitent Brothel and the sequence with the succubus have been singled out for particularly unfavourable comment. To an extent this criticism is understandable: Brothel's speech at the opening of act IV does jar, its expression of moral shame at variance with the mood of what has gone before. What is more interesting, though, is what is actually being said. It is a deeply misogynistic speech in which Brothel identifies women as the cause of the loss of a man's soul:

> Nay, I that knew the price of life and sin,
> What crown is kept for continence, what for lust,
> The end of man, and glory of that end
> As endless as the giver,
> To dote on weakness, slime, corruption, woman!
> What is she, took asunder from her clothes?
> Being ready, she consists of hundred pieces
> Much like your German clock, and near allied:
> Both are so nice they cannot go for pride,

> Beside a greater fault, but too well known,
> They'll strike to ten when they should stop at one.
>                                                    (IV. i. 14–24)

Brothel, like Harebrain, holds opinions that are the product of 'a world where males are psychologically unhealthy, and maintain that unhealth by blaming women' (Shepherd, 1981: 64). Brothel's 'repentance' is immediately followed by the appearance of 'the devil in her shape', played, presumably, by the actor who played Mrs Harebrain, though whether the audience should immediately recognise that the figure is a spirit is arguable. The scene, with its initial echoes of *Hamlet* (which must have got a laugh) moves on more in the comic grotesque style of *Dr Faustus* or the appearance of the devil disguised as a woman to Cuddy Banks in *The Witch of Edmonton*. It prefigures, too, the appearance in *The Changeling* of Isabella disguised as a madwoman to rebuke Antonio for his faint-heart and lack of clear sightedness. It *is* a difficult scene, but I think that Middleton is trying to illustrate that the succubus/woman represents the man's conception of woman-as-temptress, which he uses to explain and justify his own lust. It is the demonstration, in action, of the men's opinions discussed above. That this is not entirely a fictional, dramatic device, but true at least to certain actual experience resulting from a troubled conscience, is indicated by an entry in the diary of Nehemia Wallington in 1618:

> When his [Nehemia's] father's maid Lidia found him alone in the shop after working hours and asked him what he was doing there, he replied with the startling words: "'Who art thou, a Devil?' (for I did think the devil would come in the likeness of some maid or some beautiful woman, being so full of lust)." (Seaver, 1985: 23)

Brothel's true 'conversion' comes with his realisation that this particular image of woman is his own false creation, and that his 'salvation' lies in himself:

> When men's intents are wicked, their guilt haunts 'em,

But when they're just they're armed, and nothing
    daunts 'em.
                                        (IV. i. 92  3)

This may not answer the criticism that Middleton has failed to
absorb the ideas into the overall fabric of the play; Alexander
Leggatt, for example, thinks the succubus 'and the scene in
which it appears seem to have come from another play' (1973:
138). Such criticism, however, tends to work from the premise
that Middleton's city comedies aim at a documentary realism,
and while this is to an extent true of their subject-matter (see the
discussion of *Michaelmas Term*), these comedies, like his work in
general, draw on a range of contrasting modes of expression
employed within a single play. Thematically the scene seems to
me to fit with the guiding ideas of the play on the nature of
roles in which characters cast themselves and seek to cast others.
This may be clearer if one does not consider the scene in
isolation (though this is encouraged by its difference from what
surrounds it), and remembers that in performance a play
presents to an audience lateral connections that are more
difficult to note when reading.

The succubus scene comes in the midst of a sequence of
scenes in which Follywit dresses himself as the Courtesan,
intending to steal from his grandfather, discredit her, and so
remove the potential danger that Sir Bounteous might marry her
and so deplete Follywit's inheritance. In dressing in this way,
while voicing anti-women sentiments, Follywit's misogyny is
revealed: he uses women to his own ends and perceives them
only as sexual objects. Blinded by the sense of his own
superiority (couched in terms that show he sees himself not only
as the best, but the sole actor in the game), he fails to realise that
in a society where appearance is all, others will cast appropriate
roles for themselves and play them to their own advantage. The
juxtaposing of the scenes in this way further suggests connections between the two plot lines. Mistress Harebrain's speech
about her husband in I. ii may be seen to apply equally to
Follywit's limited vision:

My husband's jealousy,
That masters him as he doth master me,

> And as a keeper that locks prisoners up
> *Is himself prison'd under his own key,*
> Even so my husband, in restraining me,
> With the same ward bars his own liberty.
> 
>                         (104–9, my emphasis)

In this speech Middleton expresses the interesting idea that men's possessive jealousy and fear of women is constraining to themselves too, and it is this blindness to the true nature of women that leads Follywit (again, like Harebrain) to fail to see that Frank Gullman is no longer 'a woman as she was made at first, simple of herself, without sophistication' (IV. v. 56–7), but is acting a part forced on her by circumstances, and acting it better than he acts his own.


## IV


Two scenes in the Brothel/Harebrain plot illustrate how Middleton has dramatised the idea of the deception of the senses. In I. ii Harebrain (whose emotional miserliness is a counter to Sir Bounteous's profligacy) fears a 'robbery' from his home, and instructs the Watch to keep their eyes open. His own eyes – metaphorically – firmly shut, however, and having failed to recognise the (social) roles adopted by the Courtesan and her mother, Harebrain encourages the Courtesan to visit his wife. Observing them, but unable to hear what they are saying, he, like Othello, takes the 'ocular proof' without realising that Frank has deceived him with her 'elaborate action' (97). The point is made again in III. ii, though this time Harebrain can hear but not see, and is deceived by Frank's brilliant solo performance of appearing to have a conversation with a distressed Mrs Harebrain who is at that moment in another room having sexual intercourse with Brothel.

It has become something of a commonplace to praise certain Jacobean writers – and Middleton in particular – for the portrayal of their female characters, though recently, and especially by feminist critics, attention has been drawn to the essentially male viewpoint of these characterisations.[12] Nevertheless, in the context of the seventeenth century, it seems to me that Middle-

ton's plays in general show him to be alert to the ways in which
women in his society are constrained, and that he recognises
that they are driven, just as much as men, by desire for
emotional and sexual fulfilment. In many of his early plays
women are presented traditionally, or in roles partly determined
by the genre requirements, but one can see in them signs of the
complex portrayals he achieved in later work. This emerges in *A
Mad World* in Middleton's apparent awareness that men
perceiving and casting women in such narrowly focused roles as
'property' (Mrs Harebrain) or 'harlot' (Frank) is as much a
construct as the roles adopted by an actor, or the disguises used
by Follywit. The fact that women seek to break out from these
constraints does not mean that Middleton applauds their actions
or the results (Frank's 'victory' may appear to be a rather hollow
one), but it seeks to lay the blame mainly with the men, and not
to portray women as essentially lustful and deceitful.


V


It is fitting that a play that has so extensively employed the
metaphor of theatre to explore its ideas on 'role' and 'deception'
should conclude with a play-within-a-play, appropriately entitled *The Slip* (a counterfeit coin).

Follywit and his companions arrive disguised as actors and,
under the pretence of having forgotten certain vital props,
borrow a chain, a watch and a jewel from Sir Bounteous. Follywit speaks a 'prologue' in order to give his accomplices time to
escape, and leaves, only to return almost immediately since the
rest of the gang have been 'taken upon suspicion and brought
back by a constable' (V. ii. 43–4). Improvising with a brilliance
fired by desperation, Follywit 'casts' the constable as a character
in the play, while he takes the part of the justice, using the stolen
chain as the prop to signify his role and authority. The bemused
constable is derided for his attempts to speak directly to Sir
Bounteous:

FOLLYWIT: How now, constable, what news with thee?
CONSTABLE: (To Sir Bounteous) May it please your worship,
   sir, here are a company of auspicious fellows.

SIR BOUNTEOUS: To me? Puh! Turn to th'justice, you whoreson hobbyhorse! This is some new player now; they put all their fools to the constable's part still. (V. ii. 73–8)

The constable may be a bit dim, but he still sees through disguises.

The whole scene is an inversion of the truth: characters are not what they appear, and this is reflected in the language of the play-within-a-play which articulates the truth of the situation and not a fiction as the on-stage audience supposes. In this, Middleton is deliberately reflecting the position of the actual audience in the theatre, warning them not to dismiss the events of the play they have watched as merely invention. They too, he seems to be saying, can easily be deceived by the roles others choose to play. Sir Bounteous sums up his own – and the audience's – position when he says: 'Troth, I commend their wits! Before our faces make us asses, while we sit still and only laugh at ourselves' (V. ii. 164–5).

Middleton has done more than merely follow a fashion for self-reflexivity. He has explored a way to fuse the act of theatre and the act of deception (particularly through disguise) and to implicate the audience of the play in its meaning: in other words, he embodies the meaning within the form and thereby avoids the need for direct moralising. Punishments are still meted out, though this time it is the biter bit. Appropriately, Follywit has married the courtesan, having failed to discern her role. Continuing the play world/real world metaphor, Mawworm asks in dismay, trying to distinguish actuality from fiction: 'Captain, do you hear? Is she your wife in earnest?' (V. ii. 253). The 'crimes' have been in jest, but the punishment is for real, further exhorting Middleton's audience to distinguish clearly between falseness and apparent truth.

## VI

A *Mad World, My Masters* remains comparatively neglected among the canon of Middleton's plays, perhaps because it has too frequently been viewed as an intrigue comedy only, and not as a play that explores the themes of passion, deception and the attempts of men to control women, with a structure that brilliantly dramatises these ideas. It is, for me, the most complex and satisfying of the early comedies.

## 'A TRICK TO CATCH THE OLD ONE'

Although the title-page of the first Quarto edition (1608) informs us that the play 'hath beene often in Action, both at Paules, and the Black-Fryers', it belonged initially to the Paul's company. This company appears to have ceased regular playing in 1606, when the play was presumably passed on to the Children of the Chapel who (renamed the Children of the Queen's Revels in 1604) continued to play at the Second Blackfriars until the King's Men repossessed the theatre in 1608 (see chapter 6). *A Trick* is generally supposed to come late in the series of Middleton's early comedies, possibly around mid-1606, because of its skilful plotting and its similarities to Jonson's *Volpone* (1605–6) in terms of plot and characters (Gibbons, 1980: 94–101) and to Dekker and Webster's *Northward Ho!* (1605 – also for Paul's), but there is no hard evidence to confirm this dating.

I

Although the general target areas of the satire in *A Trick* remain the same as in other city comedies (the battle between young spendthrifts and old usurers over money and women), with the action set in a London presented as a dangerous and competitive city, there are some significant innovations.

Unlike *Michaelmas Term* or *A Mad World* with their multiple plots, the structure of *A Trick* is linear, with the action based on a single stratagem. The young prodigal, Witgood, has rioted away his inheritance and been forced to mortgage his lands to his uncle, Penurious Lucre. Now reformed, and helped by his former mistress (known throughout the play only as 'Courtesan') and the Host of his local inn, he plots to regain his lands – and with them his status as a gentleman. Witgood's plan is to convince his uncle that though he is betrothed to a rich widow (the Courtesan in disguise) he might lose her if he cannot offer some proof of being on a sound financial and social footing. His uncle takes the bait, and from that moment the play appears to drive itself along, spinning off further complications through the interaction of its characters rather than by the constant intervention and ingenuity of a single intriguer. Indeed, although Witgood instigates the intrigue and can, to an extent, sit back and see it furthered by the cupidity and agressiveness of others, he neither remains in control, nor avoids the play's criticism.

The plot is a masterpiece of construction. The irony of its language and action (so pervasive that no plot summary could do it justice) creates a world of façades where virtually no one is as he or she appears on the surface, and words and attitudes change meaning as the events of the play shift our – and the characters' – angle of vision.

## II

In other (earlier?) city comedies, Middleton employed a character morally or socially superior to the intriguers to hand out punishment, or contrived a radical reversal of fortunes to give some social criminal his come-uppance. In this play, however, Middleton has removed all the virtuous characters (Hoard's brother, Kix, Limber and Joyce are mainly functional), and as a result characters interact more, finally punishing each other or, through their greed and foolishness, themselves. The comment on the characters' actions and attitudes is therefore implicit – drawn by the audience and not for them. Indeed, the direct statements of 'morality' made by Witgood and the Courtesan in the closing moments of the play are given a formal quality through the use of rhyming couplets, which may suggest the inadequacy of moral tenets that are completely out of touch with the particular pressures men and women must overcome if they are to survive.

Middleton's critical method here almost entirely avoids the direct didactic statements found, for example, in *The Phoenix*, and looks forward to the approach of his later plays. These changes in dramatic method may also reveal Middleton's shifting perceptions of his society. As Margot Heinemann has suggested, 'In unsettled times it is difficult for the dramatist to organise his comedy round a single standard or norm of acceptable civilised behaviour' (Heinemann, 1982: 67).


### III


The world of the play is one in which all actions and attitudes are conditioned in some way by money. The opening speech establishes the forces that drive the society, as Witgood, away from London (in Leicestershire), takes stock of his situation.[13] He lists his lost social status, the dangers of sexual excess, the predatory nature of lawyers, the dangers (worse than the plague) that lie in wait in London for the gallant who has debts, the importance of a woman not losing her dowry and (though less so) her virtue, and, perhaps above all, the viciousness of one's next of kin. It is a cynical view of the world that the subsequent events of the play do nothing to contradict, yet some critics have commented on what seems an inappropriate tone:

> For a play that shows a fiercely competitive world of knavery, *A Trick To Catch The Old One* is surprisingly good tempered . . . the game of knavery is played with a minimum of real animosity, and without rousing in the audience any deep sense of moral outrage against the world it depicts. (Leggatt, 1973: 59)

Although I would not wish to be so certain of audience response (which is almost impossible to assess), it is true that Middleton has not invested this play with the same savagery as is found, for example, in *Michaelmas Term*, where he expresses his ideas, as Brian Gibbons has written, 'with a power more usually found in satiric tragedy' (1980: 121). Although Hoard's social pretensions are exposed and mocked, there is not the same 'class' enmity as in *Michaelmas Term* (or *A Chaste Maid in Cheapside*), nor do we ever perceive a character to be in real danger, such as we are alerted to by Thomasine's references to the 'execution' of Richard Easy.

The chicanery over a business deal that first set Hoard and Lucre at odds with each other occurred before the opening of the play, and Hoard, Lucre and Lucre's wife seem motivated as much by a simple desire to vex each other as to get more money. At the same time, however, one should not overlook the ways in which Middleton has sharpened our perception of the characters and their actions, and set their behaviour in the wider context of a society where everyone is driven by greed.

A specific example illustrates the point about the play's 'tone'. In IV. iv, Hoard soliloquises on the happiness he has gained by marrying the Widow Medler (the Courtesan in disguise) himself, 'not only a wife large in possessions, but spacious in content' (l. 5), and he rhapsodises about having acquired that perennial desire of the merchant/usurer in city comedies – the country estate:

> But the journey will be all, in troth, into the country; to ride to her lands in state and order following my brother and other worshipful gentlemen, whose companies I ha' sent down for already, to ride along with us in their goodly decorum beards, their broad velvet cassocks, and chains of gold twice or thrice double; against which time I'll entertain some ten men of mine own into liveries, all of occupations or qualities. (10–16)[14]

Although very similar to Quomodo's speech in *Michaelmas Term* (II. iii. 82–5), this lacks the sexual undertones found there. In the midst of dreaming of becoming one of the landed gentry, however, Hoard switches immediately to consider how his good fortune might be used to get at his enemy, Lucre:

> I will not keep an idle man about me; the sight of which will so vex my adversary Lucre – for we'll pass by the door of purpose, make a little stand for the nonce, and have our horses curvet [prance] before the window – certainly he will never endure it, but run up and hang himself presently. (16–21)

Although I think Brian Gibbons is right to identify the exuberance of Hoard's 'vigour and broad humour' as being in a sense attractive and part of 'a truthful portrayal' (1980: 126), and without wishing to overstress the point, I suspect there are a number of moments in performance comparable to that in IV. iv (II. ii. 40–52, for example), where the mood can be seen to switch and the animosity between the two old men deepen momentarily into more than mere comic rivalry and 'really splendid cartoon-action' (Mulryne, 1979: 15).

There are other aspects of the play that similarly keep the edge on our perception of the action. The creditors (who closely resemble Voltore, Corvino and Corbaccio in *Volpone*) extend the atmosphere of avarice in the play. They may be broadly caricatured in their obsessiveness and back-biting, but they figure in two particularly important scenes (IV. iii and iv) in which Witgood, under arrest, is beset by the creditors for their money, now he has lost the rich widow to Hoard. Witgood, improvising brilliantly, devises a scheme whereby Hoard will pay off his debts if Witgood agrees to sign a release on the Widow. The Creditors, to persuade a suddenly reluctant Witgood to sign, promise to find him 'a widow worth ten of her' (IV. iv. 198–9). Having signed, Witgood decides to test their promise:

> WITGOOD: [*Aside*] I'll try these fellows now. – A word, sir; what, will you carry me to that rich widow now?
> 1 CREDITOR: Why, do you think we were in earnest, i'faith? Carry you to a rich widow? We should get much credit by that: a noted rioter! a contemptible prodigal! 'Twas a trick we have amongst us to get in our money. (IV. iv. 270–5)

Witgood may have doubted them all along, but the fact remains that, 'hero' or not, there is essentially no difference between the Creditors' trick and his own.

This method of criticising characters and their actions by analogy is found most significantly in the three scenes involving Harry Dampit. His name associates him with the devil, the most dangerous 'old one' of all: he is referred to by Witgood as 'old Harry' in I. iv. 37, and the faithful Audrey sings that 'There's pits enow to damn him, before he comes to hell' at the opening of IV. v. Strictly in terms of the development of the intrigue the scenes contribute nothing and could be detached from the play, but what they reveal is the 'skull beneath the skin' of this grasping society, and express in striking stage images and language the disgust Middleton seems to feel for the usurer and for corrupt lawyers. The only speech of direct and unambiguous criticism in the play is Lamprey's in IV. v, in which the audience is asked to:

> Note but the misery of this usuring slave: here he lies, like a noisome dunghill, full of the poison of his drunken blasphemies, and they to whom he bequeathes all grudge him the very meat that feeds him, the very pillow that eases him. Here may a usurer behold his end. What profits it to be a slave in this world, and a devil i'th'next? (54–9)

It may be a conventional sentiment, but it is powerfully expressed by a neutral character.

In reality there is nothing to choose between Dampit, the Hoards and Lucre – an association that is made active when Hoard comes to Dampit's lodgings to invite him in the most amiable way to his wedding. Moreover, throughout the play analogies are drawn in words and images not only between Dampit and these obvious usurers, but also between Dampit and Witgood. Middleton's criticism is wide-ranging and impartial, and not withstanding his 'wit', Witgood, who addresses his mortgage deeds as 'the soul of my estate' (IV. ii. 87), is presented as essentially 'as sordidly materialistic as the professed usurers of the play' (Farley-Hills, 1988: 119).

## IV

As in all the city comedies, the world of *A Trick to Catch the Old One* is one in which virtually every human interaction is a financial transaction. Marriage is a market place: 'A scholar comes a-wooing to my niece: well, he's wise, but he's poor; her son comes a-wooing to my niece: well, he's a fool, but he's rich' (I. i. 125–7). Women are perceived by men as simply one among their other material possessions and valued as such, a point made by the release that Witgood signs, with its catalogue of Hoard's gains from the marriage to the 'Widow Medler'. Witgood promises never to lay claim to:

> any of her manors, manor houses, parks, groves, meadow-
> grounds, arable lands, barns, stacks, stables, dove-holes, and
> coney-burrows; together with all her cattle, money, plate,
> jewels, borders, chains, bracelets, furnitures, hangings, move-
> ables, or immoveables.   (IV. iv. 243–7)

Even close family relationships are perverted and subject to
market forces. As Witgood points out (the rhyme giving his
words a proverbial ring):

> He that doth his youth expose
> To brothel, drink, and danger,
> Let him that is his nearest kin
> Cheat him before a stranger.
> (I. i. 14–17)

Middleton plays throughout on puns such as cozen/cousin, and
on the double-meanings of 'aunt' (whore) and 'uncle' (to cheat),
and during their scenes together (see especially II. i) Lucre and
Witgood constantly address each other as 'uncle' and 'nephew'
to keep the disparity between their family relationship and what
is actually going on between them at the forefront of the
audience's minds.


V


Only one character in the play appears to act for motives other
than self-interest: the Courtesan. In an essay on 'The Usurer in
Elizabethan Drama', A. B. Stonex (1916) identifies what he terms
'the prodigal-usurer play', with which the genre of city comedy
has clear affinities. A feature in the development of these plays,
Stonex suggests, is the emergence of a third major character:
the rebellious daughter, who aids, and finally marries, the
prodigal/hero. Middleton presents a variant of this motif with
the use of the Courtesan, a figure who literally embodies the
interlinking of money and sex. The number of Courtesans seems
to have been discernibly increasing in this period, but unlike the
antagonistic view found in most contemporary pamphlets,

Middleton's attitude to these women is – while unsentiment-
alised – generally sympathetic (Cherry, 1973: 63).

The Courtesan in *A Trick* appears to have made Witgood her
first and only lover,[15] though now he has set himself the aim of
regaining his former status – and with it an acceptable wife in
the form of Joyce Hoard – there is no place for her. The
Courtesan not only appears to accept this state of affairs as
unavoidable, but is prepared actively to help Witgood achieve
his aim:

> there shall want nothing in me,
> Either in behaviour, discourse or fashion,
> That shall discredit your intended purpose.
>> (I. i. 72–4)

Throughout, she remains true to this promise, for, as she says:

> Though I have sinned, yet could I become new,
> For, where I once vow, I am ever true.
>> (IV. iv. 142–3)

She is even prepared to risk losing her new-found security to
help him further. Unlike Witgood, however, she is allowed no
rehabilitation or transformation. From the 'common rioter' of
the opening scenes his wit and ingenuity can restore his wealth
and social standing and allow him to marry the wife he wants.
The Courtesan, despite her wit and ingenuity (easily the equal
of his but, unlike Witgood's, not fired by self-interest), still
remains 'A common strumpet' (V. ii. 115). For a man to marry a
whore was a conventional punishment in contemporary drama,
and while the ending of the play certainly revels in first sending
up Hoard's social pretensions and then in his discomfort at
learning who he has actually married, we are still left with a
sense of the unfairness of the Courtesan's position. It is one she
herself understands, as does Witgood, whose care for her future
takes the form of advising her to marry Hoard, though as much
for his own peace of mind as for her own good:

> Wench, make up thy own fortunes now, do thyself a good
> turn once in thy days. He's rich in money, moveables, and

lands; marry him, he's an old doting fool, and that's worth all; marry him, 'twould be a great comfort to me to see thee do well, i'faith; marry him, 'twould ease my conscience well to see thee well bestowed; I have a care of thee i'faith.  (III. i. 109–14)

As the Courtesan herself says, in words, ironically, applicable both to the rich widow she pretends to be, and the penniless, abandoned prostitute she actually is:

> I must not overthrow my state for love:
> We have too many precedents for that;
> From thousands of our wealthy undone widows
> One may derive some wit.
>
> (IV. i. 45–8)

Hoard, willing to turn the joke on himself, concludes the play with a rousing couplet amidst much jollity. But characteristically of Middleton, the play never loses its edge, and the ending is tinged with a sharp awareness that while the joke is on Hoard, the laughter is bought at the Courtesan's expense.

# 3

# 'The Roaring Girl'

## I

*The Roaring Girl* was written (in collaboration with Thomas Dekker) for the Prince's Men.[1] Formerly known as the Admiral's Men (for whom Middleton had done his earliest theatre work), Henslowe's company had changed their name in 1603 when they came under the patronage of Prince Henry, King James's elder son. They performed at the Fortune Theatre, an open-air public playhouse situated north of the city in Golden Lane, Cripplegate. Built in 1600 to replace the Rose, the company's previous home on the Bankside, the Fortune was unique among the public playhouses in being square (measuring 80 feet/24 m on the outside, 55 feet/16.5 m inside) rather than polygonal. In 1621 it was destroyed by fire, rebuilt (probably in 'circular' shape), and finally dismantled completely in 1661. The builder – Peter Streete – was the same man James Burbage had employed to demolish the Theatre in Shoreditch (built 1576), transport the timber south of the river, and reconstruct it as the Globe. The contract giving Streete his instructions for the Fortune has survived, and although much of it tantalisingly tells the builder to copy what he had done the previous year with the Globe without specifying exactly what that was, it is still a major source of information on the nature of the structure of the open-air playhouses. (The contract is quoted in Gurr, 1970: 92–4.)[2]

In many ways, *The Roaring Girl* (like *A Chaste Maid in Cheapside*) retains many of the conventions of the earlier city comedies – a series of intrigues involving rich old men, young gallants, citizens and their wives, culminating in a complex deception preceding the denoument; there is extensive use of 'disguise' and 'play acting'; the setting is London; the play is rife with topographical detail and topical references; and it shows the same lively interest in the language and practices of London's underworld.[3] The change from child to adult acting company and from private theatre to public playhouse demanded certain changes in tone and angle of vision from the plays written for Paul's, but as with the city comedies, the conventions are shaped towards the demands of this particular play, and not merely routinely repeated.

II

*The Roaring Girl* has two main plot lines. The first – interweaving the characteristic city comedy themes of love and money, sex and profit, youth and age – deals with the attempt by Sebastian Wengrave to marry Mary Fitzallard despite his father's opposition to the match. Having previously agreed to the marriage, Sir Alexander withdraws his consent and threatens to disinherit his son when he realises how small a dowry Mary will bring. Sebastian aims to change his father's mind by pretending to have fallen for Moll Cutpurse (who to Sir Alexander is 'woman more than man,/Man more than woman' – I. ii. 130–1), in the hope that his father will find any wife preferable to her. Sebastian miscalculates, however, and rather than relenting, Sir Alexander embarks on a campaign literally to destroy Moll. She turns out to be more than a match for him, and with the help of Mary's father (Sir Guy Fitzallard) and a disguise trick (designed to fool the audience as well as Sir Alexander), Moll brings about both the marriage and the restoration to Sebastian of 'all those lands . . . 'lotted him' (V. ii. 83–4). The plot demonstrates Moll's shrewdness, her selfless willingness to help others (in which she resembles the

Courtesan in *A Trick*), her 'honourable' nature, and her moral integrity, which protects her from the temptations placed in her way by Sir Alexander (in IV. i, for example). The second plot concerns the attempts of a brace of indolent and hard-up gallants (Laxton and Goshawk) to seduce two city wives – Mistresses Openwork and Gallipot – and the men's eventual defeat.[4]

Except for Moll's involvement in each plot – which is extensive in the former, but confined in the latter to her dealings with Laxton – the two plots are largely discrete in terms of action. In this sense, the structure of *The Roaring Girl* recalls that of earlier Middleton plays, which were: 'built up of several sets of characters, of almost equal importance, all revolving around a central character, or situation, which ties them together: like a multi-ringed circus with a single ring-master' (Parker, 1960: 185). Increasingly in the plays written in the middle and later years of Middleton's career, however, it is a 'ring-mistress', and although he had always been concerned to present the female point of view sympathetically in his earlier dramatic work, it is from this point in his career that he begins to set women at the centre of his plays.

## III

The play's central character – Moll – is also its most distinctive feature. Although city comedies presented readily recognisable types (which, of course, the audience may have identified as specific individuals of whom we are unaware), this play is unusual in representing unequivocally on stage a person who existed in the audience's own reality – Mary Frith. Although, as the Prologue points out, she was not the only 'roaring girl' in London (the practice of cross-dressing was apparently quite extensive – Howard, 1988), she was evidently the most celebrated, and around 1610–11 seems to have been much in the public eye. In addition to *The Roaring Girl* she appeared in Nathan Field's *Amends for Ladies* (which borrows from Middleton) and was referred to in Dekker's *If This Be Not A Good Play, The Devil Is In It* and, possibly, again in Dekker's *Match Me in London*. Indeed, the real-life Mary Frith was no stranger to the stage. *The Consistory of London Correction Book* for 1611–12 records a visit she made to the Fortune Theatre:

> This day and place the said Mary appeared personally and then and there confessed that she had long frequented all or most of the disorderly and licentious places in this city, as namely she hath usually in the habit of a man resorted to alehouses, taverns, tobacco shops and also to play houses there to see plays and prizes and namely being at a play about three quarters of a year since at the Fortune in man's apparel and in her boots and with a sword at her side, she told the company then present that she thought many of them were of opinion that she was a man, but if any of them would come to her lodging they should find she is a woman and some other immodest and lascivious speeches she also used at that time. And also sat upon the stage in the public view of all the people there present in man's apparel and played upon her lute and sang a song.

Although the specific play is not named, there seems to me little doubt that it was *The Roaring Girl*, in which case the interpenetration of art and reality for that particular audience must have been startling. The woodcut on the title-page of the first edition (Plate 1) corresponds to the description of Moll given in the play. It shows Moll wearing 'the great Dutch slop' (wide, baggy breeches then much in fashion) and the 'French doublet' that she orders from the Tailor in II. ii, with the 'standing collar' (III. iii). She is holding a sword (in her left hand) and is smoking a pipe. The hat has a flower in it and her shoes are decorated with 'roses' (IV. ii). Presumably, the visual presentation was as lifelike as the players could make it, and prefigures the more extensive (and dangerous) representation of well-known contemporary figures in *A Game at Chess* (1624).

The links of stage-world and audience-world are not limited to the character of Moll, however, but are enforced throughout the play. In I. ii. 14–32, for example, Sir Alexander is supposedly describing his 'parlour' and the art collection hung there. He is actually describing the audience who are 'set down' in the 'stories' of 'galleries' where pickpockets 'thrust and leer' for their prey, and those who stand in the yard of the 'square'

# The Roaring Girle.

## OR

## Moll Cut-Purse.

As it hath lately beene Acted on the Fortune-ſtage by
the *Prince his Players.*

Written by *T. Middleton* and *T. Dekkar.*

My caſe is alter'd, I muſt worke for my liuing.

Printed at *London* for *Thomas Archer,* and are to be ſold at his
ſhop in Popes head-pallace, neere the Royall
Exchange. **1611.**

*First Edition.*

**Plate 1** Title-page of *The Roaring Girl,* 1611 (reproduced by kind
permission of the Huntington Library, San Marino, Calif.).

Fortune Theatre. Pickpockets were an occupational hazard for theatre audiences, where 'their favourite hunting ground seems to have been the amphitheatre galleries' (Gurr, 1987: 65), and the Fortune seems to have been particularly popular with them. In V. i Moll recognises a well-dressed gallant as being in fact a pickpocket ('I took him once i' the twopenny gallery at the Fortune' – 261) and commands him to make good the loss suffered by a Lord to whom she owes a favour and who had his purse stolen 'at the last new play i'the Swan' (280), a playhouse on the Bankside, south of the Thames (see chapter 5). Again the intermingling of fiction and reality is deepened by the fact that this episode seems to be based on the real-life Moll's actual behaviour. In these ways, the audience is constantly reminded of the relationship of the on- and off-stage worlds. The metaphor of the 'world as a stage' is, of course, a commonplace in the drama of the period. It is also widely employed by Middleton in various forms (game and earnest, the play-within-a-play, for example), but here as elsewhere, he does not employ the idea or its conventions passively, but for quite specific purposes.

Given these attempts to stress the fact that Moll (Mary Frith) exists in the world of the audience and not only as a fiction within the world of the play, it is significant that the authors radically contradict what the audience might expect of the character's behaviour. Whereas in *A Game at Chess* the actions and personalities of those satirised and mimicked on stage conformed to the audience's preconceptions and prejudices, the opposite is true of Moll. As Middleton is at pains to point out in the Preface to the play, the heroic portrait presented is wholly at variance with what is known about Mary Frith's actual behaviour, a discrepancy which, as I shall discuss later, would certainly have been noted by the audience.


IV


Despite her personal celebrity, it is important to recognise that Mary Frith was not a unique phenomenon. Women who dressed as men were a social reality in the period and it is necessary to set the play in the context of the critical debate their behaviour provoked.[5] The most common argument employed against them

was that for women to wear men's clothes was to turn the
world upside down, create sexual chaos and disturb the social
order. As Philip Stubbes wrote in 1583:

> Our apparel was given us as a sign distinctive to discern
> betwixt sex and sex, and therefore one to wear the apparel of
> another sex is to participate with the same, and to adulterate
> the veritie of his own kind.

Although the sumptuary laws (which regulated who could wear
what and which were intended to ensure that dress
distinguished one social group from another) had been repealed
in 1604, there seems little doubt that any trangression in such
matters was still widely perceived as a dislocation of that order
(Jardine, 1983; especially ch. 5). The controversy was widespread
and continued throughout James's reign. In 1620 the King
himself became directly involved, and in a letter dated 25
January that year John Chamberlain recorded that:

> Yesterday the Bishop of London called together all his clergy
> about this town, and told them he had express command-
> ment from the king to will them to inveigh vehemently and
> bitterly in their sermons against the insolency of our women,
> and their wearing of broad brimmed hats, pointed doublets,
> their hair cut short or shorn, and some of them stilettos or
> poinards.[6]

The issue of women cutting their hair short is raised in *Hic
Mulier: Or, The Man-Woman*, a pamphlet that appeared in 1620.
The title-page woodcut shows two women – one sitting in a
barber's chair to have her hair cut, the other being fitted in a
man's hat and plume. These 'Masculine-women', the writer
proclaims, 'are the gilt dirt, which embroiders playhouses', and
their unconventional dress is seen not only as indicative of
unconventional and promiscuous sexual behaviour ('a shame-
less liberty to every loose passion') but as a threat to the stability
both of the family and the social structure at large.
  Seven days after the publication of *Hic Mulier*, another
pamphlet appeared – *Haec Vir: Or, The Womanish-Man*. This is
a vigorous reply in the form of a debate between the

Man-Woman, now presented as a sympathetic character, and the Womanish-Man, who has been seen as representing the homosexual tendency in James's court (Rose, 1984: 377). It is a passionate defence of women's rights to personal freedom, and a scathing criticism of those who slavishly follow popular opinion without thinking for themselves. The Man-Woman is first attacked (in language not unlike that which Sir Alexander Wengrave uses of Moll) for having: 'a shorn, powdered, borrowed hair, a naked, lascivious, bawdy bosom, a Leadenhall dagger, a highway pistol, and a mind and behaviour suitable or exceeding every repeated deformity'. This time, however, she defends herself eloquently, arguing that 'Bondage or slavery is a restraint from those actions which the mind (of its own accord) doth most willingly desire', before concluding that women:

> are as freeborn as men, have as free election and as free spirits, we are compounded of like parts, and may with like liberty make benefit of our creations: my countenance shall smile on the worthy, and frown on the ignoble, I will hear the wise and be deaf to idiots, give counsel to my friend, but be dumb to flatterers, I have hands that shall be liberal to reward desert, feet that shall move swiftly to do good offices, and thoughts that shall ever accompany freedom and severity. If this be barbarous, let me leave the city, and live with creatures of like simplicity.[7]

## V

By simultaneously stressing the 'reality' of the central character, but presenting a 'fiction' in her behaviour (a discrepancy Middleton is at pains to underline in the Preface), the authors deliberately call attention to the 'role' of that character in order, I believe, to show that Moll's behaviour is precisely that – a role – and one that is forced upon her if she is to maintain her personal freedom. In other words, a specific individual is 'adapted' and used dramatically to make a more general point about the position of women in a male dominated society. Moll articulates this in her encounter with Laxton, when she points out that it is the attitudes and behaviour of men that force her to opt out and adopt male attire, and she identifies the economic basis of women's vulnerability:

> In thee I defy all men, their worst hates,
> And their best flatteries, all their golden witchcrafts,
> With which they entangle the poor spirits of fools.
> Distressed needlewomen and trade-fallen wives,
> Fish that must needs bite or themselves be bitten,
> With a worm fastened on a golden hook.
>
> .   .   .   .   .   .   .   .   .   .   .   .
>
> My spirit shall be mistress of this house,
> As long as I have time in't.
>
> (III. i. 90–6,139–40)

The deliberate challenge to the audience's preconceptions about Moll and her behaviour (emphasised by the constant engagement the play makes with its audience), is used to focus on public opinion of women such as Mary Frith, and of women in general. 'Conservative' opinion of the kind expressed by Stubbes and the *Hic Mulier* author is represented in the play predominantly (though not exclusively) by Laxton – who assumes she is a whore who can be bought (II. i. 176–9) – and by Sir Alexander Wengrave. Sir Alexander is Moll's most implacable enemy, seeing her as not only a whore and a thief, but as a threat to the very stability of society, and he actively seeks her death. In setting up a plot to tempt Moll into stealing his gold chain of office as a magistrate, Sir Alexander hopes to have her hanged:

> all hangs well, would she hung so too,
> The sight would please me more than all their glisterings.
>
> (IV. i. 36–7)

He, like Laxton, is criticised directly by Moll and by the play as a whole for mindlessly subscribing to, and so further reinforcing, social and sexual prejudices against women. As Mary Beth Rose writes: 'it is precisely this thoughtless social conformity, dramatized by his malignant intolerance of Moll, that Sir Alexander abjures at the end [of the play]' (1984: 384).

SIR ALEXANDER:
> Forgive me, now I cast the world's eyes from me,
> And look upon thee freely with mine own,
> I see the most of many wrongs before thee
> Cast from the jaws of envy and her people,
> And nothing foul but that. I'll never more
> Condemn by common voice, for that's the whore
> That deceives man's opinion, mocks his trust,
> Cozens his love, and makes his heart unjust.
>
> (V. ii. 243–50)

The audience in the theatre, aware of their own preconceptions concerning Mary Frith/Moll Cutpurse, are encouraged to review their own attitude to slanderous and hypocritical attitudes to women, and so are forced into a direct and active response to the play's argument.

## VI

The exploration of the position of, and attitudes to, women in contemporary society is not confined to the presentation of Moll. With a completely free choice in naming the character, the fact that Middleton chose 'Mary' for Mary Fitzallard is a clear indication that she and Moll (real name 'Mary') are to be viewed in relation to each other. Mary Fitzallard is a totally passive figure. Even though, unlike Moll, she wishes to marry and adopt the traditional female role (only challenging patriarchal authority by taking a husband of her own choosing), she cannot achieve her aim without masculine help. The point is perfectly underlined when she is disguised as a page-boy (IV. i), and for a brief moment her own life is a miniature of Moll's. Indeed, the complex stage image of Sebastian (male actor) kissing the 'page' (male actor playing female character disguised as male character), while Moll (male actor playing female character who dresses as a male), disguised as the 'music master' looks on, encapsulates the gender constructions the play deals in, and stresses the fact that women in this society are forced to adopt male roles in order to be active. It is a moment, too, that reminds us that Moll adopts male dress not as a disguise (as Mary does here) but in order to express her true nature and assert her freedom of choice.

The city wives, too, are forced into some sharp manoeuvring to defeat the gallants. Although they compare the young men unfavourably with their solid citizen husbands, Middleton seems to be suggesting (as he does elsewhere – in the relationship between Thomasine and Quomodo in *Michaelmas Term*, for example) that there is a direct correlation between obsession with commerce and diminished libido, and that it is the husbands' neglect that has made their wives vulnerable. The plotting comes to a conclusion in IV. ii where Laxton and Goshawk are exposed, the wives rebuking them in terms similar to Moll's attack on Laxton. The scene ends, however, in a mood of amiable reconciliation between the men that seems at odds with the energy of deception and revelation that has gone before. Goshawk is forgiven by Openwork:

> Come, come, a trick of youth, and 'tis forgiven.
> This rub put by, our love shall run more even.
>
> (IV. ii. 215–16)

and Master Gallipot almost apologises to Laxton (320–2) before inviting the foiled seducers to 'tarry and dine here' (323).

It has been suggested that 'this scene is one of the few instances in the play where the joint authorship appears to have left some rough edges' (New Mermaids edition: xxx), though it may also reflect the presence of a strong citizen element in the audience at the Fortune. But any sincerity in Laxton's claim when exposed that 'I neither have nor had a base intent/To wrong your bed; what's done is merriment' (315–16) must be undercut by the general presentation of this unprepossessing bigot, and by the fact that his previous 'repentance' to Moll in II. i was followed by his immediate return to his plot against the Gallipots. In a sense, IV. ii, which ends with a display of male solidarity and with the women in essentially the same position as before, prefigures the final scene in the play (V. ii), which also follows the pattern of a deception followed by a reconciliation. In V. ii Sir Alexander is tricked into accepting Mary Fitzallard as his daughter-in-law and, after acknowledging Moll's part in the whole business, asks her forgiveness for his blindness. The play's ending, therefore, follows closely the model of Romantic comedy: the obstruction to true love is removed and the action culminates in a mood of festival, reconciliation and the re-affirmation of order symbolised in marriage.

Moll, however, despite her central role in bringing this ending about, and the public praise of her by Sir Alexander, remains an outsider. It has been suggested that in this the play shares the attitude to the feminist free-thinker found in many of the pro-women pamphlets: that while she is admired for her principles, honesty and vigorous challenge of received opinion of women and their rights, she is still perceived as a poten-tially dangerous destabilising element in a well-ordered social structure (Rose, 1984: 388–91). This ambiguous double-think is represented in the play by Sebastian who, though he speaks well of Moll, seems fond of her and seeks her help, still utilises the world's view of her not only to manipulate his uncle's fear of the social disgrace that marriage to Moll would bring, but also to convince Mary Fitzallard that he could not possibly really be involved with Moll (I. i. 94–107).

It seems to me that Middleton is, typically and deliberately, creating a complex mood as the play ends. Although Sir Alexander 'repents', there is a sense in which it is done in the rush of relief he feels at realising Moll is not his son's bride after all, and the fragility of Laxton's earlier 'repentance' to Moll which clearly parallels this, must also undercut the moment. Although there is a resolution to the Sebastian/Mary plot, Moll's refusal to marry is, surely, a reminder that in the 'real' world of Mary Frith and the audience, such apparent changes of heart by men have to be put into action, and that many fundamental changes still remain to be made if women are to achieve greater sexual and social freedom. Moll's decision to stay unmarried until these changes are effected, projects the issues the play has dealt in outwards into the world of the audience. Like the heroine of *Haec Vir*, who would leave the city rather than compromise her beliefs, Moll (addressing each group of characters on stage in turn and, by implication, their counterparts in the audience) explains that she will stay single until:

> you shall hear
> Gallants void from sergeants' fear,
> Honesty and truth unslandered,
> Woman manned but never pandered,
> Cheaters booted but not coached,
> Vessels older ere they're broached.
> If my mind be then not varied,
> Next day following I'll be married.
>                                (V. ii. 217–24)

In his city comedies, Middleton had begun to explore the position of women, particularly through the role of the female outsider such as the courtesan figure. *The Roaring Girl*, placing a female character at its centre, represents a direct intervention in a contemporary debate on the rights of women, and in it Middleton and Dekker help 'to create new subject positions and gender relations for men and women in a period of rapid social change' (Howard, 1988: 428).

# 4
# Civic Entertainments

With the closure of the Children of Paul's company, Middleton lost the main outlet for his work. But he had never been, and would never become, a playwright who (like Shakespeare after 1594, for example) wrote for one company only, and the work he produced in the middle years of his career is characterised by its range and variety. During these years he wrote plays for a number of adult companies, for outdoor 'public' playhouses and indoor 'private' theatres, and also emerged as a major creator of civic entertainments and street pageants.

In 1604 Middleton had contributed to Jonson and Dekker's pageant for the Royal Entry of King James into London, and in 1613 he was responsible for the brief entertainment held on Michaelmas Day to celebrate both the election of the new Lord Mayor – Sir Thomas Myddleton, a Puritan and member of the Grocers' Company – and his opening of a new freshwater system for the city which was 'the sole invention, cost, and industry' of Sir Thomas's brother 'worthy Master Hugh Myddleton, Goldsmith' (263 – all page references in this chapter are to vol. VII of Bullen's edition). Despite the similarity in their names, the playwright was not related to Sir Thomas, but it is likely that it was through the new Lord Mayor's influence that he began and maintained his close relationship with the city. Later that year, Middleton was commissioned by the Grocers' Company to provide the whole pageant for Sir Thomas's inauguration.

Each year, on St Simon and St Jude's Day (29 October) the city of London celebrated the inauguration of the Lord Mayor with pageants in the streets and displays on the river, paid for by the Livery Company of which the new Mayor was a member. The commission to conceive these pageants was a prestigious and profitable one, and other leading dramatists of the time – such as Ben Jonson, Thomas Dekker and John Webster – were responsible for Lord Mayors' Shows.

Middleton called his Show *The Triumphs of Truth*, and devised a series of pageants at key points on the Lord Mayor's procession through the city streets, and on the river, which were designed to illustrate his theme: the battle between Truth and Error for the soul of the Lord Mayor. After setting out from the Guildhall the Lord Mayor encountered the first pageant at the end of Soper Lane where, following a song, he was addressed by 'a grave feminine shape . . . representing London' (236). In Middleton's city comedies 'London' was associated with vice and danger, but here the city is represented as 'a reverend mother' with 'long white hair' and on her head 'a model of steeples and turrets'. After 'London' had welcomed the new Mayor to the city, calling upon him to 'disdain all titles/ Purchased with coin' (238) and rely on his own merit and virtue, the procession, accompanied by musicians, went to the bank of the Thames where they embarked in barges for the journey to Westminster. On the river, they saw 'five islands, artfully garnished with all manner of Indian fruit – trees, drugs, spiceries, and the like' (239): entirely appropriate for an importer like Sir Thomas.

Returning to land, the Lord Mayor was met at Baynard's Castle by 'Truth's Angel on horse-back, his raiment of white silk powdered with stars of gold' and by Zeal, 'the champion of Truth, in a garment of flame-coloured silk, with a bright hair on his head, from which shoot fire-beams' (239). When he arrived in the south yard of St Paul's cathedral Sir Thomas was confronted by Error, riding in a chariot and emblematically dressed in a 'garment of ash-coloured silk, his head rolled in a cloud, over which stands an owl, a mole on one shoulder, a bat on the other, all symbols of blind ignorance and darkness, mists hanging at his eyes' (241). Error was accompanied by a striking figure representing Envy, 'eating of a human heart, mounted on a rhinocerous, attired in red silk, suitable to the bloodiness of her manners! her left pap bare, where a snake fastens'. Error tried to tempt the Mayor with promises of 'power and profit', but was driven back by Zeal 'stirred up with indignation at the impudence of these hell-hounds' (244) to make way for the entry of Truth in her chariot, dressed in white silk 'filled with the eyes of eagles' showing her wisdom, doves – 'the sacred emblems of purity' – on her shoulders, and serpents being trodden beneath her feet. The symbolism is quite straightforward, but in case any one in the crowd could not decipher it, Zeal explained the representation fully. In her speech, Truth matched Error's argument point for point, and the battle of words won, her chariot led off the Mayor's procession with 'the chariot of Error following as near as it can get' (246).

As the procession moved on, the Mayor was presented with further pageants representing the achievement of 'English merchants, factors, travellers' (men like Sir Thomas, in fact) in spreading the 'true Christian faith' (248) and reminding the new Lord Mayor of the charitable work to 'scholars, soldiers, widows, fatherless' (255) he must undertake in order to become Truth's son; the making of money is treated from a different perspective from that found in the city comedies.

Error continued its efforts to overcome Truth. In Cheapside, a curtain representing fog or mist was held down over a pageant by Error's servants – the monsters 'Barbarism, Ignorance, Impudence, and Falsehood' – which Truth commanded to be lifted to reveal London, surrounded by figures symbolising Religion, Liberality and Perfect Love. Error drew down the mist once more, and Truth once more caused it to be raised as the parade proceeded to the Guildhall where Perfect Love welcomed them to their banquet, making the meal itself part of the dramatic event.

Following the meal, the procession returned to St Paul's for a service to bless the new Mayor, Error still attempting to cover London with the 'mist'. The pageants then accompanied the Lord Mayor to his official residence in Leadenhall where, as darkness fell, London and Truth spoke their final speeches to him. Drawing on the imagery of Light and Darkness that informs the whole pageant, Truth reminded the Lord Mayor that:

> I've set thee high now, be so in example,
> Made thee a pinnacle in honour's temple,
> Fixing ten thousand eyes upon thy brow;
> There is no hiding of thy actions now,
> They must abide the light, and imitate me,
> Or be thrown down to fire where errors be.
> (260)

The Show now reached its climax as Zeal appeared, and calling attention to Error's chariot still standing nearby, received Truth's permission to destroy it:

> At which a flame shoots from the head of Zeal, which fastening upon that chariot of Error, sets it on fire, [leaving] this proud seat of Error lying now only glowing in embers – being a figure or type of his lordship's justice on all wicked offenders in the time of his government. (261–2)

Evidently this last device (a firework of some kind) was remarkable enough for its maker, 'master Humphrey Nichols, a man excellent in his art', to receive top billing in the credits at the end of the description.

*The Triumphs of Truth* was a masterpiece of civic pageantry, visually spectacular and exciting, and with a narrative tension that matched its movement through the city. At £1300 it was 'the most expensive mayoral pageant of the Renaissance' (roughly equal to the cost of building the second Globe), but was also extremely successful, 'ranking with the finest of the Stuart period' (Bergeron, 1971: 179, 186). *The Triumphs of Truth* also marked the beginning of Middleton's long association with the city, and during the following years he was involved in a further six Lord Mayor's Shows as well as a number of other civic entertainments, though his later Shows never really matched the standard of *The Triumphs of Truth*. In 1620 he was appointed Chronologer to the City of London, responsible for noting 'all memorable acts of this City and occurences thereof', and for which he drew an annual pension of one hundred nobles (just over thirty-three pounds). It was a position he held until his death.

These civic employments – which make up a substantial part

of Middleton's output – are informed by the same militant Protestant beliefs and attitudes found in the rest of his work (see chapter 9). In *The Triumphs of Honour and Industry*, for example, devised for the inauguration of Sir George Bowles in 1617 (also of the Grocers and another Puritan), Middleton included two ugly Spanish women and a Spaniard whose foolish swaggering delighted the onlookers and which sounded, Muriel Bradbrook (1981: 70) suggests, 'the first note of an increasingly anti-Spanish mood that prevailed in the City'. The Venetian ambassador who observed the Show noted that the Lord Mayor came last in the procession, traditionally the place of greatest importance. Before him went the Archbishop of Canterbury, followed by the 'earls, marquises and other lords and treasurers of the kingdom', a clear statement that the Lord Mayor was more powerful in the City than the representatives of either church or state.[1]

By the early 1620s relations with Spain were approaching crisis point. There was considerable worry in Protestant circles in city and Parliament that Prince Charles would marry the Spanish Infanta, and strong opposition to King James's policy towards Spain (see chapter 9). In 1623, Middleton again provided the Lord Mayor's Show (*The Triumphs of Integrity*, for the Drapers, to celebrate the inauguration of Sir Martin Lumley, another Puritan), which reflected the mood of rejoicing and relief that greeted Charles's return – unmarried – from Madrid. The final tableau comprised a 'royal canopy of state . . . the Imperial Crowns cast into the form and bigness of a triumphal pageant, with cloud and sunbeams' (393), reminiscent of a similar device Middleton had used in his 1613 Show, but given this time a directly topical interpretation – the mists of heresy pierced by the rays of the true gospel. Although the Show contained much praise of King James, there was also implicit criticism of, even what looks like a veiled warning to, the Crown: the first pageant encountered by the new Lord Mayor represented a Mount Royal on which stood figures representing great kings and commanders who had risen from humble origins – and overthrown monarchs.

As with the masques he wrote, such as *The World Tossed at Tennis* and *The Masque of Heroes* (both 1619), the printed descriptions that survive of these Shows undoubtedly give only pale reflections of the actual events. Perhaps because of this they tend at best to be marginalised in discussions of Middleton's work as a playwright, at worst dismissed out of hand as 'trivial' (Schoenbaum, 1956: 7). From 1613 onwards, however, these civic employments absorbed a great deal of his creative energy and to overlook them results in a very partial understanding of Middleton's work, his relationship to the City, and his political and religious standpoint. Many of Middleton's plays, from *The Phoenix* to *A Game at Chess* show the same cast of mind and modes of presentation that one finds in his civic entertainments: in his little-known play *No Wit, No Help Like a Woman's* (1611), for example, Middleton presents a wedding masque derived from his contribution to the 1604 Royal Entry, and David Bergeron has drawn specific parallels between *The Triumphs of Truth* and *A Chaste Maid in Cheapside*, suggesting that in both Middleton 'offers a moral vision of Jacobean London, revealing the dramatist's thoroughly middle-class values and concerns' (Bergeron, 1983: 133).

# 5
# 'A Chaste Maid in Cheapside'

## I

A Chaste Maid in Cheapside was probably written in 1613 (see New Mermaids edition, p. xiii), and performed the same year by the Lady Elizabeth's Men. This company – formed in 1611 – was, until 1613, based at the Swan playhouse on the Bankside. A contemporary sketch of the playhouse (known as the De Witt drawing: Plate 2) shows a circular building, mainly open to the sky, with three tiers of galleries and a tiled roof. The drawing is dominated by the tiring-house (mimorum aedes = 'house of the actors') and the stage. The former has two sets of double doors, apparently hinged to open outwards. Above these is a gallery divided into six bays, in which figures can be seen. This gallery appears to have had three uses: it provided an 'upper level' for the actors when needed (there is no such need in A Chaste Maid); it provided a location for the musicians (referred to in the stage direction preceding V. iv); and it seems likely that this gallery also provided seating for audience. Since no other audience is drawn in, De Witt may have included them here to draw attention to this as a viewing point, though as it is not clear whether the whole drawing shows a performance, a rehearsal, or is merely a general recollection, the status of the figures remains conjectural. It has been calculated that the Swan had an audience capacity of between 2000 and 3000.

**Plate 2** The De Witt drawing of the Swan Playhouse, 1596 (reproduced by kind permission of the Bibliotheek der Rijksuniversiteit te Utrecht). The building reminded de Witt of ancient Roman theatres and he accordingly identified its features using Latin terms.

Above the gallery a canopy projects out over the stage, supported by two massive, carved pillars. The underside of the canopy would probably have been painted with signs of the zodiac, stars and so on, and was known as the 'heavens' or 'shadow'. The tiring-house is surmounted by a small hut-like structure (bearing a flag with the playhouse's emblem) which probably housed winching-gear to lower and raise a chair through a trap-door in the canopy for descents to the stage. The figure appearing from a door to the right of the hut is blowing a trumpet to announce to the world that the play is about to begin.

The stage itself juts out into the yard, its dimensions probably similar to that at the Fortune, where the contract indicates a stage 43 feet/12.9 m by 27 feet 6 inches/8.3 m. The Globe stage was similar in size, whereas the stage at the Rose appears to have been smaller, in keeping with that building's overall dimensions. The stage was probably around 5 to 5 feet 6 inches/1.5 m high; according to Thomas Platter, a Swiss who visited the Swan in 1599, 'everyone can well see it all' (Nagler, 1959: 118). Although there is no evidence that the actors performed anywhere but on the stage, Peter Thomson has commented on the labelling of the yard – *planities sive arena*:

> *Planities* [flatness] is a neutral word, without theatrical reference in the Roman world, whereas *arena* is associated with the most violent and the most acrobatic of Roman entertainments. There is just a hint in the pairing of the two words that the flatness of the yard was, during de Witt's visit, used by the actors as well as the spectators. We do not know that the yard was ever used during the performances, but the possibility that it was is strong. (Thomson, 1983: 40)

Little is known of Elizabethan and Jacobean acting styles, though just as the smaller, indoor, candle-lit 'private' theatres such as the Phoenix and the Blackfriars would have encouraged and demanded an appropriate scale of performance, so the size of a playhouse like the Swan with a large audience, many of them standing, and with some of them quite a distance from the actor, would presumably have required from him a bold and demonstrative performance, vocally and physically, if he was to catch and maintain the spectator's interest.[1]

A Chaste Maid in Cheapside is the only extant play that was certainly performed at the Swan, and none of the features indicated in the De Witt drawing is incompatible with the requirements of the text. However, it is possible that Middleton originally intended the play for a children's company – the Queen's Revels – and only handed it on to the Lady Elizabeth's Men when the two companies amalgamated in 1613. He may, therefore, have had an indoor theatre in mind (the Whitefriars – see Gurr, 1970, for details) when writing, and so the stage directions – explicit and implicit – must be treated with caution. This merger of companies may also account for the large cast and, in particular, the considerable number of female roles.

## II

In contrast to the linear structure of A Trick to Catch the Old One, A Chaste Maid, like Michaelmas Term, is built around a number of plots. It is tightly structured, with the sense of a whole society infected by lust for money or sex – or both – being created by the portrayal of a number of family (or marital) units all, in some way, interlinked with one another. In much of Middleton's work, comic and serious, the family/marriage is a central device. This is no doubt in part because 'the family . . . is a subject of perennial human interest, with its appeal to fundamental instincts' (Chatterji, 1965: 106), but for a Jacobean audience the family also provided a potent and readily recognised symbol of the wider social structure, with any dislocation of the rights and mutual responsibilities of husbands and wives, or parents and children, being seen as representative of disruption in society at large. It is a metaphor that might be expected to have a particularly powerful appeal to a dramatist with Puritan sympathies, since Puritans insisted on the importance of shared partnership in marriage, and were particularly opposed to arranged, or enforced marriages. This view is well expressed in one of the widely studied tracts on the subject:

[Matrimony is] an hie, holye and blessed order of life . . .
wherein one man and one woman are coupled and knit
together in one fleshe and body in the feare and love of God,
and by the free, lovinge, harty, and good consente of them
both, to the entent that they two may dwel together, as one
fleshe and body of one wyl and mynd in all honesty, vertue
and godliness, and spend theyr lyves in the equal partaking
of all such thinges. (Thomas Becon, *Worckes*, I, quoted by
Haller and Haller, 1941: 244–5)

More broadly, marriage was seen as 'a schoole wherein the first
principles and grounds of government and subjection are
learned: whereby men are fitted to greater matters in Church or
Common-wealth' (William Gouge, *Domesticall Duties*, quoted by
Haller and Haller, 1941: 246).

### III

As in Middleton's earlier city comedies, the sets of characters
who inhabit the multiple plots tend to have only tenuous
connections with each other, and are held together by a central
character (or situation) to which they have some relationship. In
*A Chaste Maid*, the character who links all the marital units is Sir
Walter Whorehound, a knight who has fallen on hard times but
who survives by exploiting his position in the social hierarchy.
The goldsmith Yellowhammer and his wife Maudlin, a
rapaciously upwardly mobile couple, aim to add status to their
wealth and establish the Yellowhammer dynasty through the
advantageous marriages of their children. Their daughter Moll,
with a price tag of £2000, is to marry Sir Walter and so be made
a gentlewoman; their son Tim, the 'Cambridge boy', in whom
they have invested heavily to provide a status-enhancing
education, is to marry Sir Walter's 'niece' (who is, in fact, one of
his cast-off mistresses). As 'heir to some nineteen mountains'
(I. i. 128) she will bring to the Yellowhammer dynasty that most
desired commodity of the ambitious Jacobean merchant – land.
    Sir Walter needs to keep his intended marriage a secret from
another couple – the Allwits. For years, Mrs Allwit has been Sir

Walter's mistress and borne his children, all with not just the knowledge but the active support of her husband (a wittol is a 'complaisant cuckold'), who in return is spared any of the financial or emotional cares of matrimony and fatherhood. Sir Walter's attractiveness as an economic proposition to the Yellowhammers and Allwits alike is enhanced by the fact that he is heir to Sir Oliver and Lady Kix, a sterile couple who argue long and loud about which of them is to blame for their childless state, but who are clear about who will benefit unless they produce an heir:

> 'Tis our dry barrenness puffs up Sir Walter;
> None gets by your non-getting but that knight;
> He's made by the means,
>
> (II. i. 159–61)[2]

Nor are the dangers of Sir Walter's possible marriage lost on his man, Davy, if for different reasons:

> Thus I do fashion still
> All mine own ends by him and his rank toil;
> 'Tis my desire to keep him still from marriage;
> Being his poor nearest kinsman, I may fare
> The better at his death, there my hopes build
> Since my Lady Kix is dry, and hath no child.
>
> (III. ii. 241–6)

The solution to the Kix's problem is provided by Touchwood Senior, who is as fertile as Sir Oliver is sterile, and as a result, has to live apart from his wife, since:

> Some only can get riches and no children,
> We only can get children and no riches!
>
> (II. i. 11–12)

Although he demands that his wife remain chaste during his absence, Touchwood Senior finds relief for himself by impregnating country girls who are astonished at his potency, but usually discover he has disappeared when the time comes to confront him with the consequences of his equally reliable fertility.

The remaining major character is Touchwood Junior, brother to Touchwood Senior, and as in love with Moll Yellowhammer as she is with him. In a sense, Touchwood Junior's role equates with that of the 'witty gallant' in earlier plays, in that his attempt to trick Moll's parents provides the central 'intrigue' plot of the play. But it is an indication of Middleton's deepening interest in the destructive effects on individuals and society alike of unbridled appetite, that the intrigue itself is given less emphasis than the personalities of those who render it necessary. Whereas in earlier plays the mechanics of the deception were foregrounded and provided much of the audience's pleasure, it is significant that here the credit for the plot's conception and execution is given to the maid, Susan, who is relatively un-developed in this play of richly detailed characterisation.

## IV

I bring thee up to turn thee into gold, wench, and make thy fortune shine like your bright trade; a goldsmith's shop sets out a city maid. (I. i. 100–2)

*A Chaste Maid*, like the majority of Middleton's earlier comedies, is set in the city of London, but is even more full than they are of detailed topographical references and specific locations. The play opens in a shop in Goldsmiths' Row, in Cheapside, the commercial centre of Jacobean London. The shop is an apt setting and an active metaphor for a society in which sexual and family relationships are translated into financial transactions, and the opening scene deftly establishes not only the milieu of the play, but also its tone and language, exposing immediately a world of façades peopled by characters who through greed, hypocrisy and self-satisfaction are blind to all but their own desires.

The large number of properties required in the play and the attention paid to the detail of stage-dressing underline the material concerns of this society and provide a 'realistic' context

for the action. This has led some critics to overstress the
documentary nature of Middleton's work. In fact, it is part of his
satiric method to place the most abnormal behaviour in the most
ordinary setting as a means of highlighting contrasts, and to
make his characters express their outrageous views in tones of
measured reasonableness. A good example of this is provided by
the second scene of the play, beginning with the startling speech
in which Allwit identifies and catalogues the benefits of his
situation. Though long, it is worth quoting in full:

> The founder's come to town; I am like a man
> Finding a table furnished to his hand,
> As mine is still to me, prays for the founder;
> Bless the right worshipful, the good founder's life.
> I thank him, h'as maintained my house this ten years,
> Not only keeps my wife, but a keeps me,
> And all my family; I am at his table,
> He gets me all my children, and pays the nurse,
> Monthly, or weekly, puts me to nothing,
> Rent, nor church duties, not so much as the scavenger:
> The happiest state that ever man was born to.
> I walk out in a morning, come to breakfast,
> Find excellent cheer, a good fire in winter,
> Look in my coal house about midsummer eve,
> That's full, five or six chaldron, new laid up;
> Look in my back yard, I shall find a steeple
> Made up with Kentish faggots, which o'erlooks
> The waterhouse and the windmills; I say nothing
> But smile, and pin the door. When she lies in,
> As now she's even upon the point of grunting,
> A lady lies not in like her; there's her embossings,
> Embroiderings, spanglings, and I know not what,
> As if she lay with all the gaudy shops
> In Gresham's Burse about her; then her restoratives,
> Able to set up a young 'pothecary,
> And richly stock the foreman of a drug shop;
> Her sugar by whole loaves, her wine by rundlets.
> I see these things, but like a happy man,
> I pay for none at all, yet fools think's mine;
> I have the name, and in his gold I shine.

And where some merchants would in soul kiss hell,
To buy a paradise for their wives, and dye
Their conscience in the bloods of prodigal heirs,
To deck their night-piece, yet all this being done,
Eaten with jealousy to the inmost bone –
As what affliction nature more constrains,
Than feeds the wife plump for another's veins? –
These torments stand I freed of, I am as clear
From jealousy of a wife as from the charge.
O two miraculous blessings; 'tis the knight
Hath took that labour all out of my hands;
I may sit still and play; he's jealous for me –
Watches her steps, sets spies – I live at ease;
He has both the cost and torment; when the strings
Of his heart frets, I feed, laugh, or sing,
La dildo, dildo la dildo, la dildo dildo de dildo.

                                                    (12–57)

As a soliloquy, and therefore addressed directly to the audience,
it challenges the hearer to take an attitude to the speaker. The
tone is measured and assured, while what is being described is,
by most standards, monstrous. The specific detail in the speech,
with references to 'church duties', 'breakfast', 'Kentish faggots',
the view from the rear of the house over the 'waterhouse and
windmills' (visible on Visscher's 1616 *View of London*), provides
a concrete image of middle-class domesticity, which is counter-
pointed by the images of animality – 'she's even now upon the
point of grunting' – and excess. Mrs Allwit lies as if she had 'all
the gaudy shops/In Gresham's Burse about her', with enough
'restoratives' to stock a chemist's shop, and food and drink in
over-large quantities. This exaggeration acts as a mediator on
the meaning, as Middleton brilliantly allows Allwit to present
himself in terms of self-satisfaction as a man whose greed has
led him to value the getting of 'chaldron' more than children.
Allwit's speech is a perfect example of the grotesque: here
achieved by the radical contrast established between the tone
and attitude of the speech on one hand, and its content on the
other (see chapter 11).

Here, as at other key moments in the play (the watermen's
opinion of Maudlin as a mother in IV. ii, for example), the

judgement and actions of servants offer criticism of their social
superiors and provide a clear-sighted view of the true situation:

> ALLWIT:  Pray, am I not your master?
> 1 SERVANT:  O you are but our mistress's husband.
> *Enter* SIR WALTER *and* DAVY
> ALLWIT:  *Ergo* knave, your master.
> 1 SERVANT:  *Negatur argumentum.* Here comes Sir Walter, now
> a stands bare as well as we; make the most of him he's but
> one peep above a servingman, and so much his horns
> make him.  (64–9)

The visual stage image, with Allwit standing respectfully hatless
like his servants, acts as a visual metaphor of the inverted
relationship. The spectator's response is kept balanced between
laughter and criticism as the scene proceeds into Sir Walter's
arrival and encounter with the children, Nick and Wat – a
grotesque inversion of the parent–child relationship, where the
dislocation of language and action is deeply disturbing.

R. B. Parker (1960: 191) writes: 'The grotesqueness of the
scenes and characters can be funny or horrible, and often there
is a hint of both.' William Gaskill, having directed the play (at
the Royal Court Theatre, London, in 1966), expressed the
opinion that there was no black side to the comedy, but I can
hardly think of a scene in this disturbing play to which one's
response is clear-cut, with the result that the audience is constantly made aware of their ambiguous attitude to the characters
and action of the play.[3]

## V

Unlike the earlier comedies, the play is firmly placed in time,
which goes beyond the precise and detailed topical references
that help in dating the play – such as to the Watermen, and,
possibly, the extravagant lying in of the Countess of Salisbury.
Middleton sets the action of the play in Lent. This gives the
whole play an appropriate context for ironic commentary on the
unrestrained appetite of the characters, the irony enforced by the

constant use of images and words connected with animals and food, and the play on 'meat' and 'flesh' (London's main meat market, Smithfield, was located at the east end of Cheapside). In establishing this framework, the 'Promoters scene' (II. ii) is of central importance, since it embodies many of the attitudes and tactics of the play as a whole, as a baby is treated as merely a lump of meat, with the callous hypocrisy of those concerned being presented in a broadly comic (at times even farcical) manner.

The sense the play gives of the scale of such wholesale corruption in human affairs results from the presentation, in sequence, of rituals that celebrate love and generation: betrothal (seen by all except Touchwood Junior and Moll as a commercial transaction), birth (all the babies in the play are conceived in adulterous relationships – the Allwit's, the Kix's and the Country Wench's), christening (III. ii is a brilliant exposé of greed and hypocrisy), marriage (each distorted in some way) – all of which rituals are seen to be susceptible to corruption in this society through avarice and lust.

## VI

I will prevent you all, and mock you thus,
You and your expectations.

(V. iv. 63–4)

Throughout the play, Middleton presents a series of reversals of expectation. This strategy may in part be influenced by the then blossoming vogue for tragicomedy, where such reversals are often used to resolve improbable situations or even simply for the effect on the spectator. Here, however, they are seemingly designed to focus more sharply the spectator's attitude to the depth and range of inverted morality and behaviour presented in the play. For example, Yellowhammer's extreme depravity is demonstrated by his reactions when Allwit (to protect his own investment) tells him that Sir Walter has not only a mistress but children as well. Prior to Allwit's exit, Yellowhammer's response to the news is one of outrage ('O this news has cut into my heart coz' – 1. 259). Left alone on stage, he immediately changes tack:

> The knight is rich, he shall be my son-in-law,
> No matter so the whore he keeps be wholesome,
> My daughter takes no hurt then, so let them wed,
> I'll have him sweat well e're they go to bed.
> (IV. i. 277–80)

A similar moment occurs when we see the speed with which the Yellowhammers recover from the news of Moll's 'death', their only concern being what the neighbours will say and the even more urgent need to get Tim married:

> YELLOWHAMMER:
> All the whole street will hate us, and the world
> Point me out cruel: it is our best course wife,
> After we have given order for the funeral,
> To absent ourselves, till she be laid in ground.
> MAUDLIN:
> Where shall we spend that time?
> YELLOWHAMMER:
> I'll tell thee where, wench, go to some private church,
> And marry Tim to the rich Brecknock gentlewoman.
> MAUDLIN:
> Mass a match,
> We'll not lose all at once, somewhat we'll catch.
> (V. ii. 108–116)

This pattern of reversals culminates in the 'funeral', when Moll and Touchwood Junior rise from their coffins. The effect is carefully prepared: Moll's 'death' must be played for real, and it is important that the audience are unaware of the extent of Touchwood Junior's wounds, so that they have no reason to doubt the news of his death. Unlike *Michaelmas Term*, where the 'counterfeit corse' is attended by mourners 'equally counterfeit', the stage directions at the opening of the final scene may be compared with those at the beginning of Act III in Marston's *Antonio's Revenge* (the second part of *Antonio and Mellida*) in which no parody is intended. As Dieter Mehl writes:

[Middleton] presents a situation which before had been used in tragedy only, a funeral procession. . . . The music also follows the tradition of tragedy, so that for a contemporary audience the whole scene must have seemed like the last act of a particularly sad tragedy. (Mehl, 1965: 149)

In performance, the mood might be sustained and deepened by the music continuing through Touchwood Senior's oration, with Allwit's and the mourners' lines coming as responses, further stressing the abrupt change of mood when the lovers rise from their coffins.

Structurally, the play proceeds to a conventional comic ending, with loose ends being tied and culmination in marriage. But what prevents the audience from entering wholeheartedly into the cheerful spirit of it all is the knowledge of the true natures of the protagonists and the actuality that underlies the apparent resolutions. For example, Sir Oliver's deal with Touchwood Senior merely reconstructs, in essence, the Sir Walter/Allwit arrangement: as Alexander Leggatt (1973: 142) has observed, 'Only Sir Walter is thoroughly penitent, and only Sir Walter is thoroughly crushed.' In other words, although the play resolves itself theatrically, it does nothing to dismiss our unease at the values of the society presented. In this way Middleton projects the audience beyond the closing lines of the play by forcing them to decide, as it were, whether or not to accept Yellowhammer's invitation to enter his world:

> I'll have the dinner kept in Goldsmiths' Hall,
> To which, kind gallants, I invite you all.
>
> (V. v. 125–6)

# 6
# Tragicomedies: 'The Witch' and 'A Fair Quarrel'

## I

The plays of John Fletcher are not widely studied today, and are even less frequently performed.[1] In the early seventeenth century, however, working often in collaboration with Francis Beaumont, Fletcher was responsible for developing and popularising the genre of tragicomedy, which became enormously successful, particularly with the audiences at the Blackfriars indoor 'private' theatre.

James Burbage had first bought the upstairs hall of the Upper Frater in the Blackfriars (a former monastery) in 1596, and converted it into a theatre. However, protests from local residents about the nuisance that would be caused led to the Privy Council preventing the Lord Chamberlain's Men (as they were known until 1603 when they became the King's Men) from using the theatre, and so Burbage leased the space to a boys' company, the Children of the Chapel (later known as the Children of the Queen's Revels) who were allowed to play there, presumably because they performed only once a week and so were considered less likely to cause inconvenience. In 1599 the Lord Chamberlain's Men built the Globe to replace the Theatre, and in 1608 bought back the lease on the Blackfriars: the fact that this time any protest was overruled is a tangible sign of the increased status of the players in general, and Shakespeare's company (now directly under the King's patronage) in particular. For the next thirty-three years, until the closure of the theatres, the King's Men played at the Blackfriars daily (except Sundays) from October until March or April, transferring to the Globe during the summer months while the royal Court was away from London and the law-courts were not in session.

This theatre (known as the Second Blackfriars to distinguish it from another space in the building also used formerly as a theatre), though larger than that in St Paul's (see chapter 1), shared many of that theatre's characteristics. It was lit by candles, employed music (its orchestra was deemed 'the finest in London' by one patron in 1621), and its audience were all seated – in the pit, in galleries that ran round the auditorium and behind the stage at the upper level (in effect the actors performed 'in the round'), and – unlike at Paul's where there was too little space – on the stage itself.

No longer do theatre historians accept that the indoor theatres occupied by adult companies attracted an entirely different audience from the public playhouses, and when they first occupied the Blackfriars the King's Men clearly intended no distinction between their repertoire there and at the Globe. Andrew Gurr, whose *Playgoing in Shakespeare's London* is at the time of writing the most recent study of these matters, acknowledges that the 'question of a division between the popular and the privileged . . . and what playhouses it separated people into, is the most knotty item in this whole history of playgoing', but argues that the higher price of admission to the private theatre (sixpence was the lowest priced seat, as opposed to one penny to stand at the public playhouse) must necessarily have narrowed the social range of the audience indoors. He suggests that 'the main clientele must have been the privileged, principally gallants, law students, the wealthier citizens and the nobility', and he sees a gradual widening of the division of audiences until by 1642 'the social range branched from the boxes at the Blackfriars, which might contain the Countess of Essex, the Duke of Lennox or the Lord Chamberlain himself, to the nameless chimney boys and apple-wives in the yard of the Fortune or Red Bull' (Gurr, 1988: 67, 26, 79).[2]

## II

Although Fletcher did not invent the genre of tragicomedy (it is an amalgam of Italian and English forms with a genealogy too complex to trace here), in the preface to his play *The Faithful Shepherdess* he provided a famous definition:

A tragicomedy is not so called in respect of mirth and killing, but in respect it wants deaths, which is enough to make it no tragedy, yet brings some near it, which is enough to make it no comedy.

Fletcher's ideas were influenced by those of an Italian playwright and critic, Giambattista Guarini, who at the end of the sixteenth century had caused a stir in literary circles with the publication first of a tragicomedy – *Il Pastor Fido* (*The Faithful Shepherd*, 1590) – and then of a critical thesis – *The Compendium of Tragicomic Poetry* (1601). By 1602 the play was in its twentieth Italian edition. It was translated into English in the same year, and was clearly well known enough by 1606 for a character in Ben Jonson's *Volpone* to joke about English playwrights borrowing extensively from 'th' Italian' because:

He has so modern and facile a vein;
Fitting the time, and catching the court ear.
(III. iv. 91–2)

In the *Compendium*, Guarini wrote that 'he who makes a tragicomedy does not intend to compose separately a tragedy or a comedy, but from the two composes a third thing perfect of its kind'. The writer of tragicomedy:

takes from tragedy its great persons but not its great action, its credible plot but not its true one, its movement of the feelings but not its disturbance of them, its pleasure but not its sadness, its danger but not its death; from comedy he takes laughter that is not excessive, modest amusement, feigned difficulty, happy reversal, and above all, comic plotting.

The structural basis proposed by Guarini is that of comedy: a

movement from complication to apparent reversal, to additional
complication, and finally to the untying of the knot and the
averting of a catastrophe. A key point in his aesthetic argument
(and one that set it apart from the main thrust of English
dramatic criticism with its equal stress on 'instruction' and
'delight') is the prominence Guarini gave to enjoyment, his aim
being 'to purge with pleasure the melancholy of its hearers'.
According to Guarini, moral instruction belongs in church –
plays are for entertainment. The main device for giving the
audience pleasure became the use of a plot full of surprises
with, ideally, the change from bad to good fortune arising out of
the very problems that had first seemed to deny a happy
outcome, so creating the paradox of joy springing out of
apparent disaster. Along with this strategy went Guarini's desire
to control the audience's expectations: they were to be kept in
suspense, unable to see how the disaster might be avoided,
though confident that it would. *The Faithful Shepherdess*
(probably performed in 1608) was not a stage success because,
Fletcher claimed, the audience was disappointed at not finding
'a play of country hired shepherds . . . sometimes laughing
together, sometimes killing one another'. Following this failure,
Fletcher changed the structure of his plays to make them follow
a tragic course for the majority of the action, which placed
greater emphasis on the plot devices that brought about a happy
ending and manipulated even more acutely the audience's
emotional responses. The change was evidently well-judged,
since the tragicomedy became 'the characteristic Jacobean play'
(Sturgess, 1987: 6), its popularity being established largely by the
success of Beaumont and Fletcher collaborations such as *Phil-
aster* (1609) and *A King and No King* (1611).

It is not surprising, therefore, that Middleton should produce
plays in response to the current fashion, particularly when, in
1615, he began writing regularly for the King's Men, for whom
Fletcher had become the leading playwright in succession to
Shakespeare. *The Witch, More Dissemblers Besides Women, The Old
Law* (with Massinger and Rowley) and *A Fair Quarrel* (again
with Rowley) all show this influence, but they also demonstrate
that Middleton did not slavishly follow the conventions of the
form. Whereas Fletcherian tragicomedies were mainly interested
in the effects they could create, Middleton continued to make

the same moral and didactic points found in his work generally, dealing with issues of contemporary concern and, in the case of *The Witch*, political scandal.[3]

### III

*The Witch* is a startling play, rather loosely combining four plots, each a complicated intrigue in itself. The opening scene rapidly introduces two plots. In one, Sebastian, returning from the wars, discovers that he has arrived home on the very day Isabella – to whom he was previously engaged – is to be married to Antonio. The scene also sets up the plot of the revenge of the Duchess against the Duke, her husband, who insists that she pledges herself to him by drinking a toast from a cup fashioned from her father's skull. It is a practice he repeats in the privacy of the bedroom:

DUCHESS:
 Last night he played his horrid game again,
 Came to my bedside at the full of midnight,
 And in his hand that fatal, fearful cup;
 Waked me and forced me pledge him, to my trembling,
 And my dead father's scorn.
         (II. ii. 56–60)[4]

These two 'Italianate' plots are interwoven with elaborate scenes involving the witches to whom Sebastian turns to help him prevent Antonio consummating his marriage to Isabella by rendering him impotent. These 'heightened' events are matched with a further, more 'domestic' plot line, in which Abernazes (described in the cast list in the first edition as 'neither honest, wise, nor valiant'), seeks to conceal the unwanted pregnancy of the sixteen-year-old Francisca, Antonio's sister. The action of the play is supposedly set in Ravenna, but references to the Cat and Fiddle tavern, Rutney's brothel, the law terms, tobacco smoking and so on clearly suggest London, and in many ways this strand of the play is reminiscent of the city comedies.

The final act, and in particular the final scene (V. iii), illustrate the play's dominant theatrical tactics, with a sequence of revelations and unexpected (not to say incredible) twists. In V. i, Antonio confesses that he has deliberately withheld from Isabella the knowledge that Sebastian is alive:

> I was the man that told this innocent gentlewoman,
> Whom I did falsely wed and falsely kill,
> That he that was her husband first by contract
> Was slain i'th' field; and he's known yet to live.
>
> (59–62)

Retribution is not long in coming. In the first of many revelations in the final scene we learn that Antonio:

> Entering Fernando's house like a raised tempest,
> Which nothing heeds but its own violent rage,
> Blinded with wrath and jealousy, which scorn guides,
> From a false trap-door fell into a depth
> Exceeds a temple's height, . . .
>
> (V. iii. 27–31)

Hearing this news, Sebastian throws off his disguise (as Celio), revealing that he is still alive (a fact already known to the audience). At this moment the Duchess is confronted with the body of her dead husband, and confesses to murder: 'But not adultery, not the breach of honour'(103).

Almachildes, a lecherous courtier who believes he seduced her, contests the Duchess's claim, but her maid, Amoretta, reveals it was 'a hired strumpet, a professor/Of lust and impudence' (117–18) he slept with. As the Governor pronounces her fate ('Die then a murderess only' – 123), the Duke – to the audience's surprise as well as that of the characters on stage – rises up, and in a curious shift of morality (impressed by her willingness to admit murder but deny adultery), takes her again as his Duchess, and promises never again to offend her with the skull-cup.

This kind of plotting, with its mixture of surprises, some known to the audience but others played on them, shows Middleton experimenting with (but not, I believe, parodying) many of the conventions of Fletcherian romantic tragicomedy.[5] On the other hand, much of the characterisation is more complex, and the manipulations of audience response more subtle, than are often found in Fletcher, with the result that Middleton is able to use an ostensibly 'entertaining' form, and a form not noted for the sharpness of its moral perspective, in order to carry his characteristic criticism of vice.

There are some very funny scenes within which Middleton, as usual, is able to make serious points. The witch scenes are not only theatrically spectacular and exciting (and, at times, also very funny), but provide a constant metaphor for the evil of sexual lust. For all the fun and spectacle, however, it is in many ways a savage play, and in the character of Francisca (an embryo Beatrice-Joanna in a play that offers other useful comparisons with *The Changeling*), Middleton creates a chilling portrayal of a totally amoral woman prepared to dishonour and ruin her sister-in-law in order to conceal her own pregnancy.

*The Witch* appears to have all the ingredients of a Blackfriars box-office success, especially as witchcraft was much in the news. In July 1616 a thirteen-year-old Leicestershire boy accused fifteen elderly women of bewitching him. Nine were promptly hanged, and it was King James himself, on his summer progress, who examined the boy, declared him a sham, and spared the lives of the remaining six women. In the Dedication to the extant manuscript, however, Middleton complains that the play was 'ignorantly ill-fated', which suggests that it was a flop. Richard Levin has argued that '"ignorance" . . . always seems to refer, like its antonyms, to aesthetic taste. Ignorant audiences are those that cannot judge correctly, as evidenced not only by their admiration of inferior art . . . but also by their failure to admire superior art'.[6] If this is the sense in which Middleton uses the term, then it suggests that his audience were as mistaken in their generic expectations as Fletcher claimed his to have been at the early performances of *The Faithful Shepherdess*. This seems less likely in 1616 than 1608–9, however, and it may be nearer the mark to suggest that the play was withdrawn for being perceived to draw too close an analogy with the notorious Essex divorce case (and the subsequent murder of Sir Thomas Over-bury), in which Frances Howard, Lady Essex, in order to marry Robert Carr, sought annulment of her marriage on the grounds that it was unconsummated. Equally keen for a divorce, her husband agreed with the claim, but in order not to jeopardise his own prospects of marrying again, claimed that witchcraft had made him impotent only with her.[7]

The parallels between the play and the scandal certainly appear close, and it is typical of Middleton to comment on contemporary events. In this instance he could also hope to embarrass the Howard family, leading members of the Catholic faction at Court and opponents of the group led by Archbishop Abbot and the Earl of Pembroke (see chapter 9). Indeed, renewed interest in the protagonists of this infamous case, following their release from the Tower in 1622, may have suggested to him aspects of *The Changeling* some years later (see chapter 7).

IV

In many ways, the form and tone of *The Witch* is entirely appropriate for the sensational true story to which it may have alluded. In *A Fair Quarrel* (1615), written with Rowley, the theme is virtue, and the tone is accordingly very different.

The opening act (a single lengthy scene) skilfully introduces the two main plot lines. One concerns the quarrel between Captain Ager and the Colonel, which flares up after the Colonel has called Ager a 'son of a whore'. The other is set in the world of the city (it recalls many aspects of the city comedies), and deals with the attempt by Ager's uncle, Russell, to prevent his daughter, Jane, marrying the worthy but poor (and to Russell, therefore, 'worthless') Fitzallen. In both plots male honour (the duelling code in one, the values of the city in the other) is held up to scrutiny and found wanting. At the centre of each plot is a woman – Lady Ager, the Captain's widowed mother who for seven years has remained 'A widow, only married to my vow' (II. i. 110), and Jane, secretly betrothed to Fitzallen and expecting a child (I. i. 192–4) – each required by society to defend her honour but hindered by the men from doing so, and each a victim of male aggression, pride and deceit.[8]

In a third plot, there is the same pattern of insulter (Chough), insulted (Meg and Priss) and defender (Albo), and, in the Roaring School that Chough attends with his servant, Trimtram, a clear parody of the duelling code. In IV. i, for example, a brilliant scene, dizzy with the exuberance of its language, it is revealed that Roaring, like duelling, has its rules, the insults are directly parallel ('I say thy mother is a calicut, a panagron, a duplar, and a sindicus' – IV. i. 110), the rules have to be learned, and it is as much a social 'fashion'. Roaring is the 'game' of which duelling is the 'earnest'. These parallels and analogies between the three plots are developed at the levels of language and action, creating a complex and integrated pattern of commentary and criticism, and – a clear sign of the sympathetic collaboration of the writers – achieving a unity of theme within a mixture of styles.[9]

Samuel Schoenbaum (1956: 18) has observed that in writing 'an ironic drama of middle-class life, without heroism or depravity, without corpses, and almost without violence', Middleton was alone among Jacobean dramatists. As Schoenbaum acknowledges, however, the play also clearly shows the influence of the conventions of tragicomedy. Comparisons of scenes from *A Fair Quarrel* and other Middleton plays illustrate the point. For example, in the 'near death' scene of Sir Walter Whorehound in *A Chaste Maid in Cheapside* (V. i) Sir Walter's genuine fears of death and damnation are intertwined with the Allwits' appalling but bleakly comic expressions of self-interest, whereas in *A Fair Quarrel* the comic surgeon who attends the Colonel on his death-bed (IV. ii) has left the scene before the Colonel speaks, allowing the remainder of the scene to be played in a single, solemn mood that does not demand of the audience the complex, contradictory responses found in *A Chaste Maid*.

In III. ii of *A Fair Quarrel*, Jane and the audience are equally misled by the Physician's professed desire to help her, and so are equally surprised (he has been carefully set up as a sympathetic and trustworthy character in II. ii) when he reveals that what he expects by way of thanks is sex. In III. iv of *The Changeling*, on the other hand, the audience are already aware – unlike Beatrice-Joanna – of De Flores's true intentions, and so are able to observe the character's gradual realisation of the position in which her actions have placed her. A result is that the irony one associates with Middleton is substantially reduced in *A Fair Quarrel* as the disparity in levels of knowledge on which that irony depends is sacrificed to the effect of the moment.

The conclusion of the Jane/Fitzallen plot also shows the play's use of tragicomic conventions: a series of complicated twists and turns instigated – ironically – by the Physician, result in his repentance and presence at the wedding celebrations and in an unexpected *volte-face* by Russell. In other words, as Guarini desired, the happy ending paradoxically springs from that which had appeared to threaten it most.

*A Fair Quarrel* was much praised by nineteenth-century critics, though mainly for its treatment of military, masculine honour. For Algernon Swinburne, for example, writing the Introduction to Havelock Ellis's 1887 Mermaid edition of Middleton's plays, it 'stands and will stand conspicuous while noble emotion and noble verse have honour among English readers', and he, like critics before him, saw the play's centre in the portrayal of the 'chivalrous and manful agony at sense of the shadow of a mother's shame' experienced by the 'thoroughly noble and lovable' Captain Ager (xx–xxi). This view, however, as the New Mermaids editor says, 'commits the serious blunder of seeing Ager as he sees himself' and ignores the play's more critical – and therefore more interesting – portrayal of Ager's weaknesses (such as his self-centredness, his arrogance, his narrow view of women) as well as his strengths. It overlooks, too, the tension created by the pull between Ager's and the Colonel's potential for more reasoned behaviour and the code of Honour that drives them towards disaster. In III. i, for example, Ager's conciliatory tone to the Colonel, even though it stems from his belief that he does not have an honourable cause to defend after his mother, in an attempt to prevent the duel, has 'confessed' that she was once 'betrayed to a most sinful hour' (II. i. 185), shows how he *could* behave:

> I come with mildness,
> Peace, constant amity, and calm forgiveness;
> The weather of a Christian and a friend.
>
> (70–2)

It is only the comments of Ager's seconds that suggest his behaviour and language, in the context of the duelling code, are dishonourable (14–41). The scene shows how Ager and the Colonel adopt roles that force them into confrontational attitudes, so that when they do eventually fight the immediate cause has become divorced from the root cause of their quarrel. Ager articulates a powerful argument against revenge (74–89), but the Colonel, believing it to be an attempt to avoid the fight, calls him a 'base submissive coward' (111), thereby giving Ager a legitimate reason to fight ('Now I have a cause: /A coward I was never' – 113–14), and the duel proceeds.

Placing too great an emphasis on the personalities and actions of Captain Ager and the Colonel, however, may diminish awareness of the importance of the character of Lady Ager (whom Schoenbaum calls 'the most warmly sympathetic woman in the whole range of Middleton's drama' – 1956: 18). Her attempt to reconcile her protective love for her son with her own honour provides a further angle on the theme of reconciling ideal behaviour with actual circumstances. It is brought to a conclusion in IV. iii when Lady Ager, believing her son to be safe after his duel with the Colonel, confesses to him that she only lied about her chastity to protect him. Ager's reaction, however, is not to acknowledge this demonstration of her love, but to wish the Colonel a speedy recovery so that another duel can be fought over the original insult. Lady Ager is powerless: it appears that whether she tells the truth or not she will fail. Her dilemma is explored no further, however, and at this point she drops out of the play. Even though the text indicates her presence in the final scene, she does not speak: the complexities of her relationship with her son (in which F. S. Boas sees evidence of 'the sexual mystifications which continually attracted' Middleton)[10] evidently being subsumed by the exigencies of a 'happy ending'.

This conclusion, in which Ager recognises his own faults, the Colonel repents and the two men are reconciled to each other ('Fair be that quarrel makes such happy friends!' is the play's closing line), may seem sudden and psychologically unconvincing after what has gone before, with the result that: 'the tension which gives the central scenes their power is relieved, and the unsparing view of life that narrative and characterization have embodied is destroyed' (Schoenbaum, 1956: 18). But in his criticism of the 'almost pathologically intolerant attitude of the Jacobean gentry' (New Mermaids edition, xxiii) and its expression in the duel, we see Middleton again addressing an issue of specific contemporary concern, and in certain scenes (notably the two remarkable scenes between Captain Ager and his mother, II. i and IV. iii) he achieves a complexity in his portrayal of character and relationship that pushes beyond the incident-led genre of Fletcherian tragicomedy towards the depth of insight found in Middleton's later tragedies.[11]

# 7
# 'The Changeling'

## I

The licence for *The Changeling* (written with William Rowley), dated 7 May 1622, indicates that the play was 'to be acted by the Lady Elizabeth's servants at The Phoenix'. Although the company's name was the same as that which had performed *A Chaste Maid in Cheapside* at the Swan in 1613, it seems certain that this was in fact a newly formed company, and that *The Changeling* was their first production.[1]

The Phoenix was an indoor theatre converted from a cockpit in 1616–17 and situated in Drury Lane, close to the Inns of Court and the fashionable districts of Westminster and Whitehall. The theatre was owned by Christopher Beeston, who also managed the companies that performed there, and who has been described as 'probably the single most important man in London theatre' (Sturgess, 1987: 62) for the two decades that followed the erection of the Phoenix.[2]

## II

> our citadels
> Are placed conspicuous to outward view,
> On promonts' tops; but within are secrets.
> (I. i. 164–6)[3]

93

It is usually assumed that Rowley was responsible for the opening and closing scenes of *The Changeling* and for the madhouse plot. How the two writers (experienced collaborators by this time) actually worked together is not known, but the tight structure of the play overall indicates a closely shared vision.[4] The opening scene illustrates the skill with which the characters and the play's governing ideas (change, the ease with which appearances can deceive, how passion can distort reason) are established. It also offers good examples of how the audience response is controlled, made to shift between involvement and detachment, and how the spectators' attention can be focused on a three-sided stage.

The opening speech immediately hints at Alsemero's nervous and superstitious nature, rapidly sketching in the character of a man, no longer that young, for whom the experience of falling in love is both new and disturbing, an impression underlined by Jasperino's comments to Alsemero and to the audience (25–45). At the very end of the play Alsemero recalls this moment, tracing the play's arc that begins with glances in a church and ends in a vision of hell:

> Oh, the place itself e'er since
> Has crying been for vengeance, the temple
> Where blood and beauty first unlawfully
> Fir'd their devotion and quench'd the right one;
> 'Twas in my fears at first, 'twill have it now.
>
> (V. iii. 72–6)

In the play's main source, Alsemero was kept in Alicante by adverse weather.[5] In the play, as Jasperino points out, the wind is perfect, stressing Alsemero's wilful denial of the evidence of his senses in order to stay put. This is the first of the instances that run through the play dramatising the controlling idea of the power of passion to overwhelm the reason. Francis Bacon expresses the idea vividly in *De Dignitate et Augmentis Scientiarum* (1623, book II, ch. xiii):

Tigers likewise are kept in the stables of the passions, and at times yoked to their chariot; for when passion ceases to go on foot and comes to ride in its chariot, as in celebration of its victory and triumph over reason, then is it cruel, savage, and pitiless towards all that withstand or oppose it.

The Jacobeans had a system that explained this conflict (see Anderson, 1964). Briefly, they believed that the Soul, inhabiting the whole body, was itself divided into three parts. The first – the 'vegetative' soul – was shared by all living organisms on earth; the second – the 'sensitive' soul (common to humans and animals but not plants), included the senses, which responded to the world, and had the power to seek what the body needed and avoid what might be harmful. The third soul – the 'rational' soul – embraced the first two but was possessed only by humans, and, unlike the vegetative and sensitive souls, was immortal. It was this soul that ruled over the animal in Man, elevating men and women above the beasts. Reason was credited with the power to evaluate truth, not merely appearance, and so distinguish good from evil. In other words, what might appear attractive to the senses ('the mother of Desire is nothing else than apparent good' – Francis Bacon, *De Dignitate*), might be judged otherwise by the Reason, and in a well-ordered mind Reason's judgement will prevail. But if the appetite refuses to be controlled by Reason the animal in Man becomes dominant, resulting in madness. As a result, madness in Jacobean plays is not only seen as a state of sin, but is frequently represented by the transformation of human beings to the state of animals – the tiger in the chariot. As Bacon writes, 'every passion, in the excess thereof, is like a short madness, and if it continue vehement and obstinate, commonly ends in insanity' (*De Dignitate*), which in part explains the linking of the castle and mad-house plot lines.

Beatrice-Joanna expresses this idea of the connection between sight and judgement in the opening scene, and it is picked up by Alsemero as evidence of the validity of his feeling for her:

BEATRICE:
    Our eyes are sentinels unto our judgements,
    And should give certain judgement what they see;
    But they are rash sometimes, and tell us wonders

> Of common things, which when our judgements find,
> They then can check the eyes, and call them blind.
> ALSEMERO:
> But I am further, lady; yesterday
> Was my eyes employment, and hither now
> They brought my judgement, where are both agreed.
>
> (72–9)

Parallel action is used to highlight ideas. For example, Beatrice-Joanna's and Alsemero's elegant verbal by-play (108–35) is reflected by the more direct interchanges of Jasperino and Diaphanta (137–51), and in showing the surface and the actuality, this sequence is reflective of the play's larger strategies in the employment of a double-plot structure and the pairing of characters and events.

The scene also introduces the character of De Flores. Two things about him are to be noted immediately – his name (which means both 'of the flowers' and a 'de-flowerer', a taker of virginities), and his appearance.[6] He suffers from some kind of skin disfigurement that connects with the contemporary idea of the conformity between outer and inner qualities: this is the playwrights' invention – he has no such mark in the source. His arrival prompts from Beatrice-Joanna a sudden, violent, yet seemingly irrational antipathy to De Flores (93–9), that contrasts strongly with both the polite exchanges between Alsemero and Beatrice-Joanna that precede his entry and with the playful discussion of likes and dislikes she has with Alsemero (108–35) immediately afterwards. It is a sequence that foreshadows the more dangerous experiences of attraction and repulsion to come, and the rapid shifts of mood and tone in which they are expressed.

The social dimensions of the play are deftly established. Before the play opens, Beatrice-Joanna has been betrothed to Alonzo de Piracquo, a more than suitable match for her socially, and one that will further the ambitions of her father, Vermandero. He completes the trio of men with whom Beatrice-Joanna's life is most closely involved, and in presenting him as an overbearing and dominating man who sees his own interests as paramount and who brushes aside the wishes of others, the authors indicate some reasons why Beatrice-Joanna thinks and acts as she does.

By the end of the first scene the location, characters and governing ideas have been set up. These aspects of the play are (as one would expect with Middleton), set within a closely defined social structure, and it is precisely our awareness of these social pressures reacting with shrewdly drawn individual personalities that creates the pervasive sense of 'realism' in the play, and which the playwrights are able to contrast so productively with other modes of expression.

## III

> the conception of Desire is always in some unlawful wish, rashly granted before it has been understood and weighed; and as the passion warms, its mother (which is the nature and species of good), not able to endure the heat of it, is destroyed and perishes in the flame.
>
> (Francis Bacon, *De Dignitate*)

The second act opens with a soliloquy (6–26), in which Beatrice repeats many of the ideas on the links between sight and judgement from I. i, as she addresses the audience directly on the merits of Alsemero and her own clear-sightedness in recognising his worth:

> Methinks I love now with the eyes of judgement,
> And see the way to merit, clearly see it.
>
> (13–14)

The speech reveals the way in which her mind works: how her determination to achieve what she desires prevents her from working out fully the implications of her actions. At this point she has three problems to solve: how to avoid marriage to Alonzo, gain Alsemero and rid herself of De Flores's unwelcome attention. Furthermore, having failed to stall her father's plans for the wedding, the situation is exacerbated by the shortage of time she has to play with; as she says, 'some speedy way/Must be remembered' (23–4). At this stage, the character will probably

be viewed sympathetically by the audience – her position
similar, for example, to Moll Yellowhammer's in *A Chaste Maid
in Cheapside*: a young woman denied the freedom to choose her
own husband, but forced to accept one of her father's choosing.
The key turning point for Beatrice-Joanna is when – frightened
that Alsemero, characteristically offering to challenge Alonzo to
a duel for her hand, might be killed or imprisoned – she links
the three problems together in one solution:

> Blood-guiltiness becomes a fouler visage,
> [*Aside*] – And now I think on one.
> (II. ii. 40–1)

Her decision to use De Flores (and later Diaphanta) demonstrates her belief that her social inferiors are there merely to
serve her own ends, to be bought as she would buy any other
commodity. In thinking she will call the tune she underestimates
De Flores and ignores the fact that he might have desires and
goals of his own. She also, fatally, overestimates herself, believing that she has both the right and the ability (she refers to her
'art') to control other people and events. As it turns out, she is
always one step behind De Flores, who has overheard her
conversation with Alsemero and who, unlike Beatrice herself, is
able to predict the consequences of her actions:

> I'm sure both
> Cannot be served unless she transgress.
> (II. ii. 58–9)

In the first section of the scene (70–117) we observe Beatrice,
as it were, from the outside, and – through his asides – share De
Flores's efforts to understand exactly what she is driving at.
Once that has been established, we shift our point of view to
observe him, and share – through Beatrice-Joanna's asides – her
attempts to understand his reaction, more sudden and complete
than she could have expected. The scene is one of mutual and
self-deception. This is located in the language – the different
ways in which the characters use and understand the word
'service', for example – and in their totally different notions of
the nature of the intended payment. Their passion, though

focused differently, makes them equally blind: she exits believing she has put an end to her problems; he remains, in a state of sexual excitement, savouring the rewards to come.

The climax of the pact between De Flores and Beatrice comes in III. iv. The scene begins (like II. ii) by establishing the current states of mind of the two main characters – particularly necessary in a play which uses interleaved, separate (though reflective) plots. In a short soliloquy (10–17), Beatrice restates her belief that the death of Alonzo will, through her 'wisdom', have brought her that 'freedom' she so desires. She is able to separate herself from any responsibility for the deed done by De Flores, and she still talks of 'the refulgent virtue' of her love.

De Flores, however, convinced after II. ii that Beatrice has fully understood the nature of the 'sweet recompense' he expects in payment, enters in a state of excited anticipation. In II. ii, the characters moved along parallel lines, blind to each other's thoughts, feelings and intentions, while the audience observed the actuality. The action of this scene is to open the character's eyes to things as they really are, and to resolve who will dominate whom. The opening of the scene may reveal to the audience Beatrice-Joanna's ignorance of the true meaning of De Flores's sexually charged language, but it is not until she actually offers him 3000 gold florins that he realises the misunderstanding and sees the need to make his intentions absolutely clear. Now it is Beatrice who, like Alonzo in the dark and twisting corridors of the castle, is in a 'labyrinth' (71) and at De Flores's mercy. Her delight at the opening of the scene is gradually replaced by the comprehension of what he intends, and this shift is dramatised in the way her confident speeches are replaced by short lines and asides. Conversely, his increasing dominance in the scene is reflected in his growing share of its language, and by the move from ambiguous to direct statements of his sexual demands:

> I have eas'd
> You of your trouble, think on't, I'm in pain,
> And must be eas'd of you.
>
> (97–9)

Beatrice's reaction is to reject his demands with every

argument she can muster. All are in keeping with what we know
of her character, as she attempts to stand on her dignity and
class. She promises to forget the moment if he never speaks so
again; she threatens not to forgive him his rudeness; she
reminds him of the social gap that separates them – all to no
avail. De Flores first spells out the truth of her situation:

> Push, fly not to your birth, but settle you
> In what the act has made you, y'are no more now.
> You must forget your parentage to me:
> Y'are the deeds creature;
>
> > (134–7)

before finally brushing aside her last, desperate attempt to buy
him off with the awesome lines:

> Can you weep Fate from its determined purpose?
> So soon may you weep me.
>
> > (162–3)

For Beatrice-Joanna it has become a nightmare. For De Flores,
however, the fantasy he voiced at the close of II. ii has become a
reality he can enact, as now, almost gently, soothingly, he takes
her in his arms.

BEATRICE:  Vengeance begins;
    Murder I see is followed by more sins.
    Was my creation in the womb so curst
    I must engender with a viper first?
DE FLORES:  Come, rise, and shroud your blushes in my
    bosom.  (163–7)

## IV

> . . . *the progress of Desire from its first conception is of this*
> *kind . . . it seeks hiding places and keeps itself secret . . .*
> *until throwing off all restraints of shame and fear . . . it*

*either assumes the mask of some virtue, or sets infamy itself at defiance.*

(Francis Bacon, *De Dignitate*)

From this point in the play, Middleton and Rowley concentrate on tracing the results of Beatrice-Joanna's actions, which appear to Alsemero to 'blast a beauty to deformity' (V. iii. 32) and bring about the 'change' in her from a seemingly free agent to the 'deed's creature' (III. iv. 137), culminating in Beatrice-Joanna's recognition of herself as a 'changeling' (V. iii. 149–55), and of her true nature.

Following the degrading events of the virginity tests (IV. i and ii; see below), the Fifth act opens with Beatrice waiting impatiently for her surrogate, Diaphanta, to leave Alsemero's bed. Throughout the play, her sense of values has appeared distorted (even De Flores is bemused by her ability to engage him to murder a man but be horrified at the sight of the victim's severed finger), but just how ingrained her lack of self-knowledge and belief in the disposability of other people has become is made clear in her opening speech (V. i. 1–11), which offers a good example of how soliloquies (like asides) modify the degree to which an audience engages with or detaches itself from a character. The speech is given emphasis by being 'framed' between the striking of bells to indicate the passing of an hour. Beatrice still talks of her 'honour', her 'peace' (4) and her 'right' (5), while expressing her intention to have Diaphanta killed just as she did Alonzo when he stood in her way. The disparity between our observation of her and her view of herself identifies the gap between her behaviour and her own perception of it. The same is true of her apparently genuine surprise in V. iii when Alsemero confronts her with the charge of adultery. She rebukes him ('oh, you have ruined/What you can ne'er repair again' – 34–5), and seeks to retire behind her 'spotless virtue' (42), before claiming repeatedly that though 'your love has made me/A cruel murd'ress' (64–5), she has remained true to his bed. In *The Witch*, a play that compares interestingly with this in terms of content and approach, the final confession by the Duchess (that though she has been a murderess she has remained chaste) results in her husband forgiving her and taking her again as his wife. The differences in these moments offer a good example of the essential difference between tragedy and tragicomedy.

Much of the strength of the play lies in the fact that while the authors in no way excuse Beatrice-Joanna's actions or attitudes, they demonstrate that circumstances release aspects of her personality and that these, combined with De Flores's increasing control of her, are what lead to action. De Flores himself reminds her of those things that have conspired against her:

> All things are answerable, time, circumstance,
> Your wishes, and my service.
>
> (III. iv. 22–3)

De Flores, on the other hand, has courted damnation knowingly, identifying early in the play the tension between his reason and his desire:

> Some twenty times a day, nay, not so little,
> Do I force errands, frame ways and excuses
> To come into her sight, and I have small reason for't,
> And less encouragement; for she baits me still
> Every time worse than other, does profess herself
> The cruellest enemy to my face in town,
> At no hand can abide the sight of me,
> As if danger or ill luck hung in my looks.
>
> (II. i. 29–36)

Even though De Flores is committed to his actions in a way that Beatrice-Joanna is not, he too is forced to suppress the tangible indications of his guilt (the appearances of Alonzo's ghost, for example, or the blood on his collar that will not wash out completely, but is still 'perceived'), and to take a conscious decision to press on, driven by passion. 'I will not question this' (V. ii. 34) he says when he sees Alonzo's 'wounds/Fresh bleeding' (V. ii. 32–3) in Tomazo's eye, and the conviction that he wants nothing more from life than the pleasure of Beatrice's 'honour's prize' (V. iii. 167), culminates in his finally taking first Beatrice-Joanna's, and then his own, life.

The final scene (again Rowley's) draws the castle and madhouse plot lines together and fuses them, making active the

allusive parallels that have been drawn through the preceding
action. Alibius has brought his madmen to perform a masque at
the wedding of Beatrice-Joanna and Alsemero. Alsemero, however, has not only become Beatrice's 'keeper', but wishes her
and De Flores to:

> rehearse again
> Your scene of lust, that you may be perfect
> When you shall come to act it to the black audience
> Where howls and gnashings shall be music to you.
> (V. iii. 114–17)

Beatrice-Joanna's true, inner deformity is at last revealed, and
when she finally locates her fate with De Flores, she seems to
acknowledge not just the power he exerted on her from the first,
but her own ability to defile those around her:

> O come not near me, sir; I shall defile you.
> I am that of your blood was taken from you
> For your better health. Look no more upon't,
> But cast it to the ground regardlessly;
> Let the common sewer take it from distinction.
> Beneath the stars, upon yon meteor [De Flores]
> Ever hung my fate, 'mongst things corruptible;
> I ne'er could pluck it from him.
> (V. iii. 149–56)

Here she identifies herself as the central 'changeling' of the
play's title, a word that for the Jacobeans subsumed many
meanings. It could mean a person given to change; a half-wit; or
a woman who has had sexual intercourse; but most commonly
was used to refer to an ugly or deformed child supposed to
have been substituted by fairies for a normal child they had
stolen (as in A Midsummer Night's Dream). Significantly, however,
as Dale Randall has pointed out, the word in the seventeenth
century could also have the meaning of a lamia, a devil in the
shape of a woman, and while there are others in the play who
have changed or been substituted (Alsemero, Diaphanta), and
though Antonio (the 'changeling' of the play's cast list) has
played the role of half-wit, it is clear to us and to Beatrice-

Joanna herself that it is she who is the true changeling in the play, and that from the start she has been 'a different person from the one she is taken (from the badges of birth and beauty) to be'.[7]

*The Changeling* is built on a structure of antitheses, ironically inverted and juxtaposed: castle/asylum, madness/sanity, reason/passion, appearance/reality. The final scene reproduces the variety of tone and response that has been employed throughout in these contrasts, and in the moments of black humour in the play, such as De Flores producing the severed finger, the ghost showing his finger missing during the wedding dumb-show, or the death of Diaphanta. Here, the final appearance of Beatrice-Joanna and De Flores is set against lines between Alsemero and Vermandero which, though clearly not intended by the characters to be comic, are equally clearly intended to be taken as such by the audience:

VERMANDERO:
  Oh, Alsemero, I have a wonder for you.
ALSEMERO:
  No, sir, 'tis I have a wonder for you.
VERMANDERO:
  I have suspicion near as proof itself
  For Piracquo's murder.
ALSEMERO:
          Sir, I have proof
  Beyond suspicion for Piracqo's murder.
VERMANDERO:
  Beseech you, hear me; these two have been disguised
  E'er since the deed was done.
ALSEMERO:
          I have two other
  That were more close disguised than your two could be
  E'er since the deed was done. . . . (121–9)

and so on, until Tomazo's exasperated interjection ('How is my cause bandied through your delays!') will, I suspect, undoubtedly and intentionally raise a laugh. If so, it will be rapidly curtailed first by Beatrice-Joanna's cries from off-stage (which may possibly complicate an audience's response still further[8]), and then by the appearance of De Flores with Beatrice-Joanna's wounded body.

It is important to question why the dramatists employ these tactics. The simultaneous presence of contradictory moods is a defining characteristic of the Grotesque (see chapter 11), and one of its intended effects is to prevent an audience from identifying too closely with and losing themselves in the action – the switch of responses keeping them detached. On one level this enables us both to share and evaluate Beatrice-Joanna's death (she is in part to be pitied, in part condemned), but it may also enable us to maintain a clearer viewpoint on other characters. It creates, I think, a tension between the mood of closure (the lessons to be drawn from the protagonists' deaths) and the attitude we take to other surviving characters.[9]

Following Alsemero's synopsis of the play's action in which he again catalogues the prolixity of changes that have occurred, we observe a closing of the male ranks. As his daughter dies, Vermandero's greatest concern is for his own reputation:

> Oh, my name is entered now in that record,
> Where till this fatal hour 'twas never read.
>
> (180–1)

Alsemero is on hand to comfort him, however, and to offer himself as a substitute, living, male child (though no 'changeling'):

> Sir, you have yet a son's duty living,
> Please you accept it; let that your sorrow,
> As it goes from your eye, go from your heart;
> Man and his sorrow at the grave must part.
>
> (216–19)

These are, to a degree, the conventional demands of closure, and the play operates as a standard Jacobean tragedy in demonstrating that the penalty for sin is death and damnation. But Middleton is invariably unwilling to see matters in quite such straightforward terms, and in these closing moments he complicates the issue accordingly. Although not guilty, of course, in the same way as Beatrice and De Flores, Vermandero

and Alsemero are upholders of codes and expectations that
define women and prescribe their lives, and if we baulk at the
way they close ranks here, it is nevertheless entirely consistent
with their personalities and social roles as presented in the
play.[10]


# VI


Kenneth Muir has written that: 'It is difficult to praise too highly
Middleton's psychological realism with regard to the main
characters.' (*Thomas Middleton: Three Plays*, 1975: xiv). It is the
very complexity of the 'psychological' portrayal of character,
and the consequent stress placed upon these 'realistic' elements
in the majority of discussions of *The Changeling*, that have
highlighted two aspects of the play that have been widely
criticised: the 'mad-house' plot and the 'virginity test' in act IV.


## The 'Mad-house' Plot

The world of the castle is reflected in a world of more obviously,
though no more genuinely, mad people. No direct source for
this plot has been identified, but a section of Reynold's story
discarded for the main plot contains the situation of a jealous
husband who confines his wife and sets a spy to watch her,
which may have suggested the parallel of Alsemero and Alibius.
    In the last two scenes of the play (V. ii and iii) the two worlds
are brought together physically with the presence of the inmates
and their keepers at the intended celebrations of the marriage of
Beatrice-Joanna and Alsemero. Although only three of the
remaining twelve scenes are given exclusively to the mad-house,
their presence and influence are felt throughout the play, acting
as a reflection of the main action, furthering and deepening its
themes, as those living in a world of apparently 'normal'
relationships behave with a 'real and terrible madness that leads
to the death of four people, while in the world of apparent
madness sanity always manages to assert itself, so that no real
damage is done' (Revels edition, lxvii).

The tone of the mad-house plot is to a large extent comic, though a modern audience's responses to this will be hampered by the usual problem of understanding Jacobean verbal humour when we do not know what all the words mean, and because we do not – unlike large numbers of Jacobeans – find madness funny (Thomas, 1977). Of all the mad-house scenes, the first (I. ii) is the most directly comic in intention, and despite the reservations just made, it succeeds in laying the necessary basis of the links with the main plot, and (like the opening scene of the play), establishing location, characters and circumstances. A further complication is provided by our likely failure to distinguish between Antonio and Franciscus, and the important distinctions the playwrights draw between fools (such as Antonio pretends to be) who are so from birth, and madmen (like Franciscus) who go mad as a result of events and experiences in their lives. (See Daalder, 1988, for a full discussion of the play's notions of 'madness'.)

The second mad-house scene (III. iii) introduces Isabella, the young wife of Alibius, the mad-house keeper. The parallels between her situation and Beatrice-Joanna's are immediately obvious: two young women, spirited and resourceful, but subjected to the will of men. The difference between them, of course, lies in the way they respond to their situation.

The interlinking of the plots and the reflections of characters, situations and ideas, are achieved through a framework of allusions, echoes and parallels in language and actions, and one example must serve for many. In IV. ii, Alsemero 'tests' Beatrice-Joanna's virginity and, unaware that she has deceived him, believes that what he sees is the truth. In the following scene the situation is inverted as Isabella disguises herself as a mad-woman and makes sexual advances to Antonio, who tries to brush her aside ('Pox upon you; let me alone!' – 118). When she persists, and in desperation he cries to her 'I am no fool,/You bedlam' (125–6), her rebuke serves to remind him that he should not place such reliance on the capacity of outward appearances to provide absolute proof:

But you are, as sure as I am, mad.
Have I put on this habit of a frantic,
With love as full of fury, to beguile

The nimble eye of watchful jealousy,
And am I thus rewarded? [*Reveals herself*]
ANTONIO:
                    Ha, dearest beauty!
ISABELLA:   No, I have no beauty now,
Nor ever had, but what was in my garments.
You, a quick-sighted lover? Come not near me!
Keep your caparisons, y'are aptly clad;
I came a feigner to return stark mad.

                                        (126–35)

The scheme of the two scenes is clear: Beatrice-Joanna's feigning conceals the truth, Isabella's reveals it, and such counterpointing of scenes and smaller units of action is characteristic of the relationship of the plots throughout the play.

The second part of the scene (following Isabella's exit) presents a problem of a different sort. Apparently determined to get his own back on both Antonio and Franciscus, Lollio sets them against each other, and it seems likely that a fight will result. This never materialises, however, and it may be that a scene resolving many of the events in the mad-house is missing, though I suspect that in performance the audience's attention focuses increasingly on the resolution of the Beatrice/De Flores/Alsemero action.

### The Virginity Test

The theme of chastity is central to the play, and is focused on the virginity test itself (IV. i and ii). The action stresses the importance of virginity in a bride (in performance Beatrice-Joanna may well still be dressed in her wedding gown), adds dramatic tension (will her secret be discovered?), gives dramatic form to the kind of deceitful cover-up her initial action has inexorably led her to, gives further example of her easy and instinctive use of her social inferiors as her tools, and in paralleling Alsemero with Alibius as physicians, helps further to integrate the two plots.

Even allowing for these dramatic functions, some critics have found the specific event itself too far fetched, describing it variously as 'fantastic', 'preposterous', 'ridiculous', 'absurd' (in the sense of 'ludicrous'), and so on. A seventeenth-century audience may well have viewed things differently, however. Such tests were by no means unknown, and treatises by respected scientists were widespread: for example, in *Eighteen Books of the Secrets of Art and Nature*, published in 1660 in an augmented form, the author, Dr Read, quotes a number of experiments for discovering a virgin, all of which involve drinking or urinating or both (Randall, 1984).

The 'virginity test' might have had an added *frisson* for its original audience, however.[11] I have already referred to the close similarity between the plot of *The Witch* and the events surrounding the Essex divorce case in 1613 (see chapter 6). One of the key moments in the hearing had been the examination of Frances Howard in order to ascertain whether she was the virgin she claimed to be. She was required to submit to a physical examination by two midwives and four ladies of the court, who found her to be a virgin. She had been involved for some time with her lover, Robert Carr, however, and it seems extremely unlikely that they had not consummated the affair. Many were unconvinced at the findings. Archbishop Abbot thought the jury had been bribed, but popular rumour was that Frances had substituted a virgin for herself:

> The Countess being ashamed, and bashful, to come to such a Tryal, would not expose her Face to the Light; but being to appear before the Matrons under a Veil, another young Gentlewoman, that had less offended, was fobbed into the Place; and she passed, in the Opinion, both of Jury and Judges, to be a Virgin.

There can be little doubt that this notorious event is being referred to when Diaphanta, being quizzed about her virginity by Beatrice, says in an aside to the audience:

> She will not search me, will she,
> Like the forewoman of a female jury?
> (IV. i. 100–1)

In other ways, too, the plot of *The Changeling* rehearses the

events of the Essex divorce and the connected murder of Sir
Thomas Overbury, and Middleton seems to have responded to
the rekindled interest in the case caused by the release from the
tower of Frances Howard and Robert Carr in January 1622, only
four months before *The Changeling* was licensed.[12] In 1614 he
had contributed an entertainment – *The Masque of Cupid* (now
lost) – to the marriage celebrations of the Earl and Countess of
Somerset, and the rapidly revealed disparity between the public
face and the private truth of Overbury's murder may have
touched his ever-keen sense of irony. It may certainly have
suggested to him that in their play, he and Rowley could give
life to the vivid metaphor employed by Sir Francis Bacon at
Lady Frances's trial:

> the theatre of God's justice . . . hath a vault, and it hath a
> stage: a vault, wherein these works of darkness were con-
> trived; and a stage with steps, by which they were brought to
> light.

# 8
# 'Women Beware Women'

## I

The earliest printed edition of the play is dated 1657, and was issued bound together with another Middleton play, *More Dissemblers Besides Women*. Although the two titles may have suggested a likely combination to the publisher, and although it has been suggested recently that both plays deal with issues of topical polititical concern, the plays are very different in tone. *More Dissemblers*, written around 1615, is one of Middleton's tragicomedies (see chapter 6), whereas *Women Beware Women* is a sharp analysis of the inextricable links between power, sex and money. In this it more closely resembles Middleton's early comedies, and Margot Heinemann's description of it as a 'city tragedy' is apt.[1]

The edition was prefaced by a short commendatory verse by Nathaniel Richards, a Puritan and playwright, in which he observed that:

> I that have seen't can say, having just cause,
> Never came tragedy off with more applause.
> (11–12)

Exactly where and when this performance took place is not

known, and suggestions for dates of composition range between
c. 1613 and c. 1621. My own view is that the maturity of the
style and the play's angle of vision are indicative of the later
part of Middleton's career.

II

The first act presents the two 'worlds' of the play – city and
court – the interaction between which provides the mainspring
of the action. It establishes that in both worlds emotions and
actions are subject to parental and economic pressure (there is
hardly an action in the play that is not a result of, or motivated
by, class and money), locates characters in their social milieu,
and introduces the ideas (women as possessions, the tension
between pleasure and business, the tug between pragmatism
and emotion) that underpin the play overall.

The opening scene is set in the modest home of Leantio and
his widowed mother. Leantio's occupation (he is a 'factor', a
kind of Jacobean travelling salesman) defines his class status in
the play – he is the only person who works for his living. Just
back from a business trip to Venice, and accompanied by a new
bride, Leantio is torn between pride in his new 'purchase' (12)
and fear that 'his treasure' (14) whom he has stolen from her
parents 'great in wealth, more now in rage' (50) may in turn be
stolen from him. She must, he reasons, be locked up. Leantio's
mother, with an awareness of class distinction (that helps
explain her inability to resist Livia in II. ii), and with her
judgement unclouded by passion, is alert to the problems her
son's marriage may lead to:

> What ableness have you to do her right then
> In maintenance fitting her birth and virtues?
> (I. i. 65–6)[2]

Throughout these exchanges Bianca remains silent, but the
groupings of the characters amid items of simple, plain furniture
(in contrast with those in the scenes set in Livia's home and the
court; note how carefully Middleton details these in IV. i), would
presumably have combined with costume, vocal and physical

performance to present a stage image that demonstrated the radical difference between Bianca and her new circumstances.

When Bianca eventually speaks (at l. 125), her courteous and rhythmical language conveys a sense of her upbringing. Her speech has a proverbial tone ('There is nothing that can be wanting/To her that does enjoy all her desires'; 'I am as rich as virtue can be poor'; 'he that traffics much drinks of all fortunes'; 'The voice of her that bare me is not more pleasing'), and though there is nothing to indicate that these statements are voiced insincerely, the language may suggest to the audience that Bianca's sentiments are as yet untested by experience.

The second scene – set in the home of the aristocratic widow, Livia – continues the theme of marriage, as Guardiano, Fabritio and Livia discuss the proposed match between Guardiano's idiot Ward, and Fabritio's daughter, Isabella. The discussion centres on the balance between passion and reason in love. Livia articulates the progressive view that women should not be forced into unsuitable marriages, but soon after sets about an elaborate deception aimed at persuading Isabella to marry the Ward. Thought, feeling and action are dislocated in Livia at this stage. This not only underlines the casual pragmatism that pervades the court, but lays the ground for the journey that Livia – like Bianca – must take in order to find her proper 'place'. When she falls in love with Leantio (in III. iii), only to see him murdered by her brother (IV. ii), she is no longer able to divorce feeling and action, but can then unite them only in the act of revenge.

Left alone with Hippolito, Isabella (as Bianca does later) addresses the audience on the dilemma of women forced into loveless marriages, and used as commodities in the economic dealings of their fathers. It is a theme common in Jacobean drama, and one that from *The Phoenix* on remains central to Middleton's work as a whole:

> Oh, the heartbreakings
> Of miserable maids, where love's enforced!
> .  .  .  .  .  .  .  .  .  .  .
> By'r Lady, no misery surmounts a woman's:
> Men buy their slaves, but women buy their masters.
>                                       (I. ii. 166–7,175–6)

The positions of Bianca and Isabella are clearly paralleled in the play; I think we may speculate that Bianca has eloped with Leantio to escape just such an arranged marriage (the Mother comments in I. i that 'her fortune . . ./At the full time, might have proved rich and noble' – 59–60). Both women enter into relationships in which 'passion' and 'reason' are separated: Bianca with Leantio, who is both socially and emotionally unsuitable for her; and Isabella with the Ward, who is witless. They both have to say 'farewell' to 'all friendly solaces and discourses', and have to turn to adulterous and incestuous relationships to find the self-fulfilment denied them by their families. Given these pressures, it is psychologically convincing that Bianca should embark on such an apparently lop-sided marriage and that Isabella (in II. i) should cling immediately to the seemingly improbable revelation that Hippolito is not her uncle. Even then, although she believes that Hippolito is no longer a taboo lover, the enforced marriage to the Ward still condemns Isabella to an illicit relationship – adulterous though not incestuous – which must be kept 'hid from sin-piercing eyes' (238).

At the end of the play Bianca acknowledges her part in her own fate and her betrayal of her marriage vows (V. ii. 202–11). She also claims that women's chief enemy is other women and that 'Like our own sex, we have no enemy' (215). This traditional view of the essential wickedness of women (put, interestingly, in a female character's mouth) is challenged and undercut, however, by the presentation in the play of equally vicious manipulations by men, and of the social practices such as arranged marriages that deny women freedom. As in other plays, Middleton is showing that women are in many ways the victims. The audience will undoubtedly find Bianca's analysis here less than complete, and may perhaps take her reference to her 'own sex' to mean that it is the very fact of being female that exposes women to danger.

At the opening of the third scene, Leantio, whose only experience of the kind of leisure enjoyed by 'great gallants' is when 'many holidays' come together, identifies the differences between his life and theirs:

Those that are wealthy, and have got enough,

> 'Tis after sunset with 'em; they may rest,
> Grow fat with ease, banquet and toy and play,
> When such as I enter the heat o' th' day.
>
> (I. iii. 31–4)

But his reason sets other guidelines:

> But love that's wanton must be ruled awhile
> By that that's careful, or all goes to ruin:
>
> (41–2)

Leantio's linking of the place of passion in public and private matters may act as a motto for the play:

> As fitting is a government in love
> As in a kingdom; where 'tis all mere lust
> 'Tis like an insurrection in the people,
> That raised in self-will wars against all reason.
>
> (43–6)

It is at this precise moment – Leantio leaving for work, Bianca left alone in the house with her mother-in-law – that the two worlds collide, as the Mother and Bianca see the Duke in procession. The 'great solemnity' of the stage procession is significant since it not only offers Bianca (from the mundane work-a-day perspective of her marriage) a glimpse of the life for which she was more likely intended, but in making the Duke notice her while involved in a 'yearly custom and solemnity,/ Religiously observed' (82–3), Middleton indicates the façades of the world of the court, where behind the outward show ''tis all mere lust'.

### III

> When I am in game, I am furious; . . . I think of nobody when I am in play, I am so earnest.' (I. ii. 98–102)

In *The Changeling*, Middleton and Rowley used the mad-house plot to parallel and comment on the characters and events of the castle plot. In *Women Beware Women*, although the shared experiences of certain characters are made clear, the structure of the play differs in that it traces a number of separate story-lines that are linked thematically (punishment for sexual depravity, male domination of women, the corruption of the court and so on), and by the intervention of Livia in each plot line. At the same time, however, the characters of the Ward and Sordido are used as a kind of fairground mirror in which the behaviour of the superficially respectable characters is revealed in its true distortion. In III. iii, for example, the elegant dance between Isabella and Hippolito is matched by the grotesque parody of the Ward dancing with Isabella, an image which makes concrete the true nature of the young woman's relationship with her uncle, and in III. iv the essential quality of the marriage market is revealed as Isabella is paraded like a horse being sold.

Throughout the play, the active image of the 'game' is employed, culminating in the great court game of the masque. Widely employed by Middleton in his work, this is a traditional dramatic device with its origins in English medieval drama, whereby the 'game' (the play) is the means by which the 'earnest' – or actuality – is revealed. Therefore, the play *Women Beware Women* as a whole is a 'game' that comments on the actuality of the lives of the audience watching it, while the 'game' elements within the play reveal the actuality of the lives of its characters.

Understood in this way, the use of the Ward and Sordido's games as 'comic parallels' clearly stems from more than Middleton's desire to vary tone and mood. Such variety may well be a result, and the play will benefit, but it is not the main purpose: the image of the shuttlecock batted between the two rackets, for example, is an apt one for the position of Isabella specifically and Bianca more generally (II. ii).

A more developed image is that of the chess game in II. ii. In comparison to the physical nature of the Ward's games, chess – a cerebral game of strategy in which minor pieces are sacrificed to protect major ones, in which the Queen (the quean–whore pun is set up earlier in the scene) is the most manoeuvrable piece on the board, and 'mating' the King is the object of the game – is a sharply appropriate parallel for the events of the scene. Moreover, with the pieces corresponding broadly to the social hierarchy represented in the play (and Jacobean society at large), it offers a controlling metaphor for the play overall.

It is important to note the physical stage image. The chess game is played on the main stage, while the actuality (the 'earnest') is acted out on the upper level. The audience, therefore, is able to perceive both levels of action simultaneously, with Livia's and the Mother's comments (the former's knowing, the latter's innocent) acting as a commentary on the action above, ensuring that we are kept alert to the true nature of the Duke's manipulative actions:

> LIVIA:  Did not I say my Duke would fetch you over, widow?
> MOTHER:  I think you spoke in earnest when you said it, madam.  (388–9)[3]

## IV

Roma Gill has described *Women Beware Women* as 'the finest of all Middleton's works' (1983: 36). Many other critics agree, though her further judgement that 'the characters are consistent and convincing', finds less general acceptance, at least where the portrayal of Bianca is concerned. The problem centres on what some see as too radical a change in the character of Bianca following her visit to Livia's house. The Revels editor (who also quotes a range of other views) writes: 'The new Bianca is unrecognizable as the same girl who entered the play's opening scene', and suggests as part of the reason, 'the moral pressure exerted by a society's habit of mind; Bianca, moving from outside the play-world into its midst, becomes – perceptively and movingly – the novice fully initiated into the corrupt society' (lxvi–lxvii). What should be stressed, however, is the exact nature of this initiation – for the ceremony here is rape. When she re-enters on the main stage (in II. ii) Bianca's language – charged with images of disease, infection, rottenness – embodies the violence of the assault on her. She *is* different, and the change in her relationship with Livia and with Leantio's Mother is evidence of her changed position in the play.

Although the Mother finds Bianca 'strangely altered' (III. i. 7), the audience knows exactly what has happened to her. Where we can be less certain, however, is in our knowledge of her previous character against which to measure this 'alteration', since we have little to go on other than her few and formal words in the opening scene, and her thrill at being noticed by the Duke. At the opening of the play the emphasis is on the fact that Bianca is a stranger in that household. She is connected to it only by the tenuous links of a marriage of which the causes (escape from her parents and, possibly, an arranged marriage) and the actuality (confinement in the house with a mistrustful older woman) have both been made perfectly clear. Indeed, the Duke's temptation – a mixture of cajolement and threat – stresses the tawdry surroundings in which Bianca now lives:

> Do not I know y'have cast away your life
> Upon necessities, means merely doubtful
> To keep you in indifferent health and fashion –
> .   .   .   .   .   .   .   .   .   .   .
> Come, play the wise wench and provide for ever;
> (II. ii. 375–7, 382)

and it is precisely this lifestyle that is the target of her first words in III. i:

> Why is there not a cushion-cloth of drawn work,
> Or some fair cut-work pinned up in my bedchamber,
> A silver-and-gilt casting-bottle hung by't?
> (19–21)

Bianca's rape has not liberated her: she is as much a possession as she was of her parents and then Leantio. She, as much as Beatrice-Joanna, is 'the deed's creature', but the deed at this stage is not of her doing.

## V

The journies of Bianca, the Mother and Leantio from the city to the court are completed in III. iii. From this point in the play the action is located there entirely. It is set against activities emblematic of the court's values – the banquet, the code of honour and the masque – and the contrast Middleton draws between the ideal and the actuality of these identifies the deep-rooted corruption of the ruling class. We are shown not only how relationships are perverted by the pressures and temptations to which the characters succumb, but also what happens when true feeling confronts strategy, and it is this collision in particular that forms, I think, the dominant theme of the remainder of the play.

III. iii is a key scene, and offers shifting perspectives on characters and events, most particularly in the presentation of Leantio. Whereas (apart from one soliloquy, IV. i. 23–40), Middleton shows little of Bianca's innermost thoughts, concentrating on what happens to her and so stressing how little freedom she has, his portrayal of Leantio is much more complex. Although the character is at times manipulated by the author in an almost schematic manner (the opening and closing speeches in I. iii, for example), Middleton also presents the character with an objective detachment, shifting the audience's perspective and attitude. The sympathy we may feel for Leantio on losing Bianca is rapidly modified by his excessive reaction to lock her up even more securely in a room that has no windows on the world. On the other hand, some understanding for the character is engaged by the obvious pairing of Leantio with the Ward. Both men are merely pawns in others' games and can only watch as their respective 'wives' are taken by other men. The Ward is half-witted, while Leantio sees himself as 'like a thing that never was yet heard of,/Half merry and half mad' (III. iii. 52–3): each must 'give away his part' (225) in the bedding of his bride.

The moment when Livia first sees Leantio (an echo of the Duke's first sight of Bianca) marks another turning point in the play, since she never

> truly felt the power of love
> And pity to a man, till now I knew him –
> (61–2)

Up to this moment all relationships have been seen to be 'political' or transitory, expressed through images of sexual gratification and mercantile value, and Livia's seduction of Leantio significantly offers a mirror-image of the Duke's temptation of Bianca. The moment is highly charged: Leantio's mind is 'Still with her [Bianca's] name' (308) and he fails to hear Livia's blandishments. She exits, recognising that "'Tis as unseasonable to tempt him now/So soon' (314–15) and that Bianca's 'strange departure stands like a hearse yet/before his eyes' (318–19), leaving Leantio to trace the hardening of his attitude: if he is to be a cuckold, then he might as well be a wealthy one. Livia returns to the stage after his soliloquy to announce to the audience that:

> I have tried all ways I can, and have not power
> To keep from sight of him.
>
> (349–50)

It is a convention of Elizabethan and Jacobean drama for characters to move through states of mind more rapidly than a modern actor may find comfortable, but here it is more indicative of the strength of feeling that overrides Livia's more usual pragmatic nature. Her temptation of Leantio recalls his mother's lines at the opening of the play. Now Leantio has sacrificed all for money, Livia all for love, and the similarities and differences of their actions are summed up in the shifting meanings of the repeated word 'enough' as they close the deal:

LIVIA:  Do you but love enough, I'll give enough.
LEANTIO:  Troth then, I'll love enough, and take enough.
LIVIA:  Then we are both pleased enough. (374–6)

If at the beginning of the play Leantio was the merchant he has now become the commodity.

This clash of the desire for wealth with 'true feeling' is demonstrated at key points in the following act: in IV. i Leantio and Bianca swop boasts of their material gains, the shared lines of their verbal fencing emphasising the similarity of their ambitions. He loses because he still cares, while her closing lines display her total lack of feeling for him, and Leantio's final, pathetic attempt to defend himself in a real fencing match with Hippolito ends in his death. Livia is stung into action by the discovery of Leantio's death at the hands of her brother Hippolito. When she kneels before Hippolito and Isabella and

speaks of the return of her 'sense and judgement' over her 'rage
and distraction' (IV. ii. 169–70), there is a significant difference
between their and our understanding of her meaning.


V

In time of sports, death may steal in securely  (V. ii. 22)

The game metaphor that pervades the play in language and
action provides the framework for the final scene of the play.
Earlier in the play Livia issued a challenge to the audience:

> Who shows more craft t'undo a maidenhead,
> I'll resign my part to her.
> (II. i. 178–9)

and throughout, characters have concealed their true feelings
and actions behind adopted roles. The choice of a masque in
which to conclude the play's action, therefore, has an internal
coherence in that it sustains the 'play-acting' that has preceded
it. As Guardiano says, expressing the failure of characters to
acknowledge their own responsibility for their actions:

> mischiefs acted
> Under the privilege of a marriage-triumph
> At the Duke's hasty nuptials, will be thought
> Things merely accidental, all's by chance,
> Not got of their own natures.
> (IV. ii. 162–6)

As the great court game, a masque is a fitting climax to the play,
but although a modern audience will respond to its formal
appropriateness, they may miss its particular political significance. As a symbol of the power of the court and of the ruler,
the masque 'presents the triumph of an aristocratic community;
at its centre is a belief in the hierarchy and a faith in the power
of idealization' (Orgel, 1975: 40). Orgel notes that 'as a genre, it
is the opposite of satire; it educates by praising, by creating
heroic roles for the leaders of society to fill', and so Middleton's

presentation of a scene of chaos and accidents operates as a tangible symbol of a corrupt and chaotic court. Contemporary censorship laws forced Middleton to adopt the convention of a foreign setting for the play, but Margot Heinemann is surely right in thinking that the London citizens who saw it 'are very unlikely to have taken the play as a fantasy picture of exaggerated Italian vice' (1982: 193).

The scene is a brilliantly sustained irony, with characters' parts and deaths sharply fitted to their roles in the preceding action: Livia is cast as the marriage goddess, for example, and Bianca takes a poisoned kiss from the Duke. The blood-bath is set against a disorientating comedy (drunk pages getting the cups mixed up, Guardiano falling – literally – into his own trap, the Duke despairingly trying to follow the synopsis in his programme while Fabritio complains that they are not doing it properly) that serves to emphasise the bizarre chaos of these rotten lives. It is apt that the Duke receives his 'wound' first but dies last – a reflection of the arc of corruption he has spread over the whole play.[4]

The events draw out from the characters confessions that, as Hippolito says, 'Lust and forgetfulness has been amongst us,/ And we are brought to nothing (V. ii. 146–7), as each identifies his or her particular crime. Interestingly, however, Middleton has used a spokesman for morality in the play in the figure of the Cardinal. We are used to seeing cardinals in Jacobean plays (in *The Duchess of Malfi*, *The White Devil* or *'Tis Pity She's a Whore*, for example) as corrupt hypocrites, but although he fails to change his brother's ways, and has to suffer a lesson in morality from Bianca (IV. iii. 47–69), these events stress the immorality of others rather than fault in him. It is the Cardinal (associated with light as the Duke is associated with darkness), who has the last word, identifying the final stage-tableau of carnage as a warning emblem:

> Sin, what thou art these ruins show too piteously.
> (V. ii. 222)

Despite the internal and external appropriateness of this startling final scene, it has been harshly treated, mainly by critics who approve when they think Middleton writes like a 'Jacobean

Ibsen', but are less happy with the radical disorientations of the Grotesque.[5] It is not only reader-critics who are at fault here. In the programme that accompanied Howard Barker's 'collaboration' with Middleton to produce a 'new' *Women Beware Women*, Max Stafford-Clark asserted that the masque is 'unperformable and rather silly'. There is no doubt that, even leaving aside the technical difficulties of staging it, the scene presents considerable problems in a modern production since without knowing what a masque represents the full political significance will be lost. It is a view that, in my opinion, has recently been proved wrong by John Adams's production at the Birmingham Repertory Theatre in 1989, which demonstrated not only the feasibility of staging the scene today, but how its radical contrast with the style of the opening scenes embodies the journey to chaos and destruction that Middleton's characters have traced.[6]

# 9

# 'A Game at Chess'

## I

From his earliest published poem to his last play, Middleton's work reflects his militant Protestantism, frequently expressed in terms of an antipathy towards Catholics in general and Spain and Jesuits in particular. In this it follows in the tradition of chauvinistic works such as John Foxe's *Acts and Monuments of the Christian Reformation* (popularly known as *The Book of Martyrs*) and the *Book of Homilies*, a collection of sermons on topics such as 'Order' and 'Obedience' written by Elizabethan bishops to be read in churches. These and other Protestant writings stressed the political dangers of Catholicism, portraying England as an Elect Nation engaged in battle with a Catholic church identified as a whore and headed by a Pope identified as the Antichrist. Catholicism's complex ritual and ceremony was savagely attacked and parodied, especially what was seen as its worship of idols and images 'all for eye, and to snare the heart of a carnall man, bewitching it with so great glistening of the painted harlot' (quoted in Dures, 1983: 82). Catholicism, it was claimed, was not merely a misguided form of Christianity, but had debased and perverted Christ's teaching in order to justify its followers' pursuit of sensual pleasure. In the words of the

Puritan writer William Perkins: 'Of all religions, to the carnal man none is so pleasant as popery is.'[1]

In 1611 the Master of the Revels (the government censor), Sir George Buc, licensed for performance the anonymous play *The Second Maiden's Tragedy*, which I believe to be by Middleton. This startling play cast the struggle between Protestant and Catholic in the form of a battle between Govianus, the rightful ruler, and the Tyrant who has usurped his throne, for the Lady to whom Govianus is betrothed. To avoid being taken by force by the Tyrant, the Lady (she is given no name) begs Govianus to kill her, but he fails, and she takes her own life. In the action that follows, the purity of Govianus's veneration of the Lady's spirit is contrasted with the Tyrant's idolatory of her dead body. The Tyrant exhumes the Lady's corpse, clearly with necrophiliac intentions, and hires a painter – actually Govianus in disguise – to paint her face so that it looks to be alive. Govianus paints the lips with poison and – in a scene that strongly echoes the murder of the Duke in *The Revenger's Tragedy* – the Tyrant dies as he kisses the corpse's lips. Govianus is restored to his throne and the spirit of The Lady returns to unite with her corpse and praise Govianus for his steadfastness.

Although the more sensational moments of the play appear to owe something to the blossoming vogue for tragicomedy (and the sequence of the painting of The Lady and her reappearance offers a bizarre echo of the climax of *The Winter's Tale*), its basic intention – to present an allegory of the threat posed by popery to Protantism and to England – was entirely serious. It is one of a number of plays that resulted from (and no doubt contributed to) a wave of particularly virulent anti-Catholic feeling that swept the country at the time, which had been growing since the alarm caused by the Gunpowder Plot in 1605 and been fired by the assassination in 1610 of Henri IV of France, an act for which the Jesuits were widely believed to be responsible.

In 1611, King James appointed a new Archbishop of Canterbury, George Abbot, described by one Catholic as a 'brutal and fierce man and a sworn enemy of the very name of catholic'. In 1612, Abbot wrote to the Archbishop of York that James wished the country rid of 'popish recusants', and Abbot's appointment was perceived by one Jesuit as a clear sign that the

King desired 'the extermination of all catholics', observing that 'the times of Elizabeth, although most cruel, were the mildest and happiest in comparison with those of James' (Dures, 1983: 49).

Whatever James's thoughts, however, his court still entertained many Catholics from home and abroad, and as the surviving manuscript shows, *The Second Maiden's Tragedy* was heavily censored in order not only to tone down the ferocity of its anti-Catholicism, but also to modify its satirical jibes at the dissolute nature of the court.[2]

## II

Elizabeth I had used the prospect of her marriage as one of the tactics in her foreign policy. James, himself already married, sought to use the marriages of his children in the same way. In 1613 he married his daughter Elizabeth to the German Protestant Frederick, the Elector (ruler) of the Palatinate, and pursued plans to marry his son Charles (replacing Prince Henry following the latter's death in 1612) to the Spanish Infanta, Henrietta Maria. These marriages, James hoped, would put him in a strong and peaceful position in Europe through alliances with the Protestant Union and the Catholic League, and enable him to mediate between the two sides. More practically, the dowry his son's bride would bring would help James's shaky finances. To the majority of English people, and in Parliament, the proposed match with Spain was highly unpopular, their ingrained hostility heightened first by James's refusal to intercede on Frederick's behalf when he was deposed by the Catholic army of the Emperor Ferdinand, and then by the execution of Sir Walter Raleigh at the instigation, it was widely believed, of the Spanish ambassador, Gondomar. 'It is a strange thing', wrote the French ambassador, undoubtedly with some satisfaction, 'the hatred in which this king is held.'

Sometime between 1615 and 1620, Middleton wrote *The Mayor of Queenborough, or Hengist, King of Kent*, in which he specifically referred to the dangers posed to Britain by alliances

made through marriage with foreign, non-Protestant powers.[3]
As the First Lord says at the end of the play, the nobles would
have remained loyal to their king:

> If from that Pagan wound thou'dst kept thee free;
> But when thou fledst from heaven, we fled from thee.
> (V. ii. 51–2)

Given the strict censorship, such allusions are necessarily
oblique, and Middleton protected himself further by casting
*Hengist* in the by then old-fashioned form of the Chronicle play
and setting the story in Saxon England. By the early 1620s,
however, 'the very survival of protestantism in Europe seemed
to be at stake' (Dures, 1983: 82), and opposition to the King's
plans grew still stronger and more widespread. Middleton
touched on the issue in other works at this time. At the end of
*The World Tossed at Tennis* (1619–20), a masque he wrote with
Rowley, a Soldier announces his intention to join the volunteers
who are leaving to help Frederick:

> I'll over yonder, to the most glorious wars
> That e'er famed Christian kingdom.[4]

A. A. Bromham (1986) has further suggested that *Women Beware
Women* (1621), though not in such a direct manner, also engaged
with the issue of the Palatinate and James's policy towards
Spain.[5]

The crisis came in February 1623 when Prince Charles,
accompanied by the Duke of Buckingham, travelled in secret to
Madrid, where they were lavishly received. Despite agreeing to
a range of Spanish demands concerning the rights of Catholics
in England (conditions that would have been totally unacceptable at home), Charles failed to win any promises of help in the
Palatinate and six months later returned to London empty-
handed and wifeless – to the general rejoicing of his subjects.

An entry in his diary by Sir Simonds D'Ewes, a Puritan
lawyer and Member of Parliament, gives a sense of the mood at
the time:

During Prince Charles his being in Spain, the English Papists began to triumph insolently and to boast of a toleration they should have shortly; yea, after his return they purposed to set up a Popish lecture publicly at the French Ambassador's house in Blackfriars in London. The first sermon was preached on Sunday, the 26th day of October, in the evening, by one Father Drury, an English Jesuit, and many were very unlawfully assembled to hear him; but God Almighty, by the fall of the room, gave a stop to that begun resolution, in which Father Drury himself, and divers others, were slain outright, and many wounded and maimed.[6]

It was in this atmosphere that Middleton wrote *A Game at Chess*, the most controversial political play of the Jacobean period. For his material Middleton drew not only on his own observations and attitudes to political events at home and abroad, but on the wide range of pamphlets that appeared, particularly two by Thomas Scott, a Puritan preacher and political satirist. The first part of Scott's *Vox Populi* had been published in 1620, 'marvellously displaying', one contemporary wrote, 'the subtle policies and wicked practices of the Count of Gondomar' (the Spanish ambassador), and claiming to be a record of Gondomar's report on his political successes in England to the King of Spain. Published to coincide with Gondomar's return to England, it apparently hit its mark. The Venetian ambassador wrote that Gondomar 'foams with wrath in every direction and it is said that he has sent it to the King to make complaint'. Scott escaped to The Netherlands to avoid arrest and continued to publish his satires from there. In May 1624 the *Second Part of Vox Populi* arrived in London and was incorporated by Middleton into his play, indicating how quickly he was writing and the flexibility of the text.

*A Game at Chess* was not the only play in the 1623–4 season to satirise the Spanish and the marriage negotiations. Even away from London the business was newsworthy, and in Norwich the authorities prosecuted a member of the Princess Elizabeth's provincial company for announcing a performance of a play (now lost) called *The Spanish Contract*, which no doubt also dealt with the affair. Whether or not all this dramatic activity was 'a spontaneous reaction of the dramatists of the period against the mishandling of England's foreign policies by the court', or part of a centrally orchestrated campaign 'initiated and sponsored by a group of politicians whose goal it was to use all means available to win the support of both nobility and the commons' (Limon, 1986: 2), the aim of Middleton's play is quite clear: to capitalise on the anti-Spanish and anti-Catholic emotion running high in city and Parliament and to raise even higher the consciousness and prejudice of the broad social mix that comprised the Globe audience, including the illiterate who could not read pamphlets of the kind Middleton drew on for the play. Although by August 1624 when *A Game at Chess* was performed the immediate crisis was past (it had been licensed in June but delayed until King James left London for the summer in anticipation of the trouble it would clearly cause), the issue of a Catholic marriage was still a live one. Furthermore, the threat posed by the Arminian faction led by William Laud was seen by many to be growing, and feelings towards Jesuits in particular (against whom the play's most spiked attacks are made) were still extremely hostile.[7]

Today the play remains largely neglected as a text for study or performance, the very topicality that made it such a scandal and success proving a considerable barrier for the modern reader or spectator. Although *The Second Maiden's Tragedy* shares some of the same impulses to create racial and sectarian hatred, impulses that we find unacceptable but which run throughout Elizabethan and Jacobean drama, it (like *Hengist*) can be read today as a powerful study of tyranny and lust. This is helped by the fact that in *The Second Maiden's Tragedy* the political/religious allegory of the Govianus plot is matched with another – marked by the psychological realism of its characterisation – in which similar issues of vice and virtue are explored in a domestic context.

*A Game at Chess*, however, cannot be fully appreciated without a detailed knowledge of the events and personalities to which it refers, though the text does offer insights into the physical use of the Globe stage and the various means employed to manipulate the responses of an audience drawn from all sections of society. Since the events that followed its presentation were well documented it also provides examples and evidence of the relationship of companies, their patrons, and the authorities.

## III

The play opens with an Induction (a conversation between
Ignatius Loyola, founder of the Jesuits, and the allegorical figure
of Error), which sets the scene as England, and identifies the
enemy as specifically the Jesuits and their secret supporters, not
just the more obvious enemies of Spain and Catholicism. A
dream was also a traditional setting for an allegory, however,
and Error's lines "'Tis but a dream,/A vision you must think'
may have been intended to try to head off potential censorship
by stressing the 'artificiality' of the piece (rather like saying 'it
was only a joke' when challenged). What is more certain is that
it sets the tone and style of the play, which are in many ways
not dissimilar to the allegorical pageants Middleton had become
well known for in the city and which inform his dramatic
method in *A Game at Chess* particularly strongly. The visual
representation of Error, for example, may well have been based
on that employed in Middleton's 1613 pageant, *The Triumphs of
Truth* (see chapter 4).

The English are represented by the white chess pieces, the
Spanish by the black. As in his pageant work, Middleton makes
much of the symbolic association of these colours with light and
dark, good and evil. Many of the physical aspects of chess
appear to have been employed in the staging. It is not clear from
the text precisely how many actor/pieces there were or how
they were dressed (though obviously in black and white), but it
seems likely to me that they wore representative head-dresses of
the kind known to have been used in pageants. Entrances
were evidently marked as the Black and White 'houses' and
throughout the play, as in a game, when pieces are 'taken' they
are consigned to the 'bag' (Foakes, 1985: 122–5). Middleton
establishes the chess metaphor at the outset, relying on the
audience's recognition of it as a hierarchical game of strategy
and of its wider, analogical ramifications (chess was also known
as the 'Royal game' and the 'Spanish game'). However, although
the overall structure of the play follows the characteristic flow of
a chess game, beginning with the pawns and concluding with
the high-ranking pieces, it does not follow the rules at every
moment. While Middleton uses specific chess moves (the
'checkmate by discovery' in act V, for example), he is aware that

even those members of the audience who might recognise them are more likely to be interested in what is being done and said than in particular gambits. In other words, the rules of chess necessarily take second place to the demands of the play in the theatre. As Middleton indicates in the Prologue, his use of the game will be selective:

> What of the game called chess-play can be made
> To make a stage-play shall this day be played.
> $(1-2)^8$

with the play's ultimate aim being the audience's pleasure and approval:

> But the fairest jewel that our hopes can deck
> Is to play our game to avoid your check.
> (9–10)

## IV

The play's central, unifying plot strand is the attempt by members of the Black House – especially the Jesuit, the Black Bishop's Pawn, helped by the Black Queen's Pawn – to seduce the White Queen's Pawn. On one level, the Pawns' plot is an allegory of the Catholic (specifically Jesuit) attempt to subvert the followers of the Anglican church, represented by the White Queen's Pawn (a pattern not dissimilar to the Tyrant/Lady element of *The Second Maiden's Tragedy*). Jane Sherman suggests that this plot deals also with contemporary political events, and she sees the two 'full-house' scenes in II. ii and III. i as direct representations of the 1621 and 1624 Parliaments. She argues that in being enticed by the prospect of a marriage, the White Queen's Pawn may also represent Prince Charles, allowing Middleton (protected by reversing the sex of the protagonists) to comment on the Prince's proposed marriage and on the English royal family's propensity to be deceived by Catholic blandishments, with perhaps an oblique reference to Anne of Denmark's conversion to Catholicism. Her argument is persuasive, and though it may appear to be too obscure for all but the most perceptive in the audience, especially as so much of the play's satire is extremely blatant, we should neither underestimate the Jacobeans' readiness or ability to decode, nor forget that plays can frequently be read on a number of different levels by different groupings within an audience (Sherman, 1978).

The play's other plot line deals with the machinations of the Black Knight. This figure represented Gondomar, the Spanish ambassador who had been responsible for the major part of the marriage negotiations as well as working to keep James from intervening in the crisis in the Palatinate. According to John Chamberlain, the actors 'counterfeited [Gondomar's] person to the life, with all his graces and faces, and had gotten (they say) a cast suit of his apparel for the purpose, and his litter'. Certainly, the illustration of Gondomar on the title-page of one of the editions of the play (Plate 3) closely resembles the portrait in the Royal Collection at Hampton Court as well as other portraits and engravings (Foakes, 1985: 122–5). The title-page illustration of the character of Antonio de Dominis (the Fat Bishop in the play) is extremely close to other pictures of the real man, so it seems likely that the actor (Middleton's frequent collaborator William Rowley) was made up appropriately. Similar attempts may well have been made with other 'pieces' intended to represent specific people, such as the White King's Pawn (the disgraced Lord Treasurer, Lionel Cranfield, Earl of Middlesex) and the Black Duke (Count Olivarez). The White Knight and White Duke must have been recognisable as Charles and Buckingham, though this may have been evident from their actions as much as from their costumes. The White King would obviously be immediately associated by the audience with James, which would have presented Middleton with a more particular problem, since one of the strictest embargoes on the stage was the representation of the monarch. Indeed, as it turned out, it was this that formed the core of the charges against the company and author when the play was suppressed.

The two plot lines are established in the opening scene and closely linked throughout the play. It is made clear that the Black Bishop and the Black Knight are both engaged in striving for 'universal monarchy' – the former on behalf of Catholicism in general, the latter specifically in pursuit of Spain's own territorial ambitions. They represent, therefore, the spiritual and

**Plate 3** Title-page of the undated first Quarto of *A Game at Chess*, probably published in 1625 (reproduced by kind permission of the Huntington Library, San Marino, Calif.).

temporal enemies of England and Protestantism. By enmeshing
the strands so closely (there are few scenes that keep them
discrete) Middleton's structure demonstrates that the forces that
threaten England are inextricably intertwined, and for that
reason especially dangerous.


# V


The fifth act concentrates on Prince Charles in Madrid, though
Middleton tactfully makes the purpose of his visit his attempt to
save the White Queen's Pawn rather than to arrange his own
marriage to the Infanta. In V. i, Middleton dramatises the
apparently warm welcome given to Charles and Buckingham,
but underlines the idolatory and ritual associated with
Catholicism (the 'erroneous relish' as the White Knight terms it),
with which they wish to ensnare him. Using an elaborate stage
device of an altar with images that move in a dance, Middleton
portrays the Catholic Mass in terms of magic and idolatory, and
since a number of the audience can have had no real knowledge
of such ceremonies, the play is actively creating for them a
stereotype of Catholicism.

Throughout the play the Black House prides itself on its
ability to dissemble (through language and dress) and its ability
to conceal this deception. At the same time the members of the
Black House are shown to be given to boastful self-revelation, as
in the Black Knight's speeches in IV. ii. It is a mixture of deceit
and arrogance that brings about their downfall in both plots. In
V. ii the Black Bishop's Pawn, still aiming at the downfall of the
White Queen's Pawn, is fooled by a bed-trick and the Black
Queen's Pawn exposed (in a very funny scene) for her lechery.[9]

In the final scene, the White Knight and White Duke 'feign a
little' to lure the Black House into a false sense of security, and
so allow the Black Knight enough rope to hang himself. After
admitting to a number of vices and being reassured that these
present no problems in the Black House, the White Knight owns
up to his greatest sin – that he is 'an arch-dissembler'. He is,
ironically, speaking the truth, but the Black Knight walks

straight into the trap, admitting to the White Knight – and to the thousands in the playhouse – that:

> what we have done
> Has been dissemblance ever.
> (V. iii. 158–9)

It is the final 'discovery' of the play, and Middleton puns on the chess gambit of 'checkmate by discovery' – on one level a move where two pieces work together to mate the opposition, on the other the fatal self-discovery of the Black House – to draw his brilliantly sustained metaphor to an end.

At this moment the White House arrives and the Black pieces are driven into the 'bag'. The Spanish ambassador (who had not seen the play, but had heard reports) described the moment: 'The Prince of Wales . . . beat and kicked . . . Gondomar into Hell, which consisted of a great hole with hideous figures.' The bag has been referred to earlier in the play, but its identification here specifically with the traditional 'hell mouth' makes clear the allegory and underlines that the action of the play represents not only the struggle between the Elect Nation of England and Spain, or Protestantism and Catholicism, but the fundamental battle between God's people and the Antichrist, between heaven and hell.


## VI


The Epilogue is a very clear guide to the play's ways and means. Just as the Induction establishes the links between the stage and audience worlds (a relationship further enforced by the White Queen's Pawn in V. ii), so do the closing lines, spoken directly to 'this assembly'. Looking around the theatre the actor warns that any who might be Jesuit or Catholic sympathisers:

> Where'er they sit, stand, and in corners lurk,
> They'll soon be known by their depraving work.

It must have been a brave man or woman who did not join enthusiastically in the applause.

## VII

The impact of *A Game at Chess* was immediate and enormous. It opened on Friday, 6 August 1624, and 'was Acted nine days together' to packed houses at the Globe. John Chamberlain wrote that the production was: 'frequented by all sorts of people old and young, rich and poor, masters and servants, papists and puritans, wise-men etc., churchmen and statesmen'.[10]

It was not to prove popular with everyone. After seeing the second performance, one George Lowe wrote that the general opinion of this 'new play . . . which describes Gondomar and all the Spanish proceedings very boldly and broadly' was that 'it will be called in and the parties punished'. The prediction proved accurate. Although the King was away from London for the summer, the Spanish ambassador's protests soon reached him, the play was suppressed, and the theatre closed. The main charge against the actors was that they had contravened the 'commandment and restraint given against the representing of any modern Christian kings'. Despite Middleton's efforts to portray James favourably, it was the opinion of the Venetian ambassador that while the 'Spaniards are touched from their tricks being discovered', the 'king's reputation is much more deeply affected by representing the case by which he was deceived' and that 'they will at least punish the author'.

The actors were called before the Privy Council on 18 August to explain themselves, but as they were able to show that the play had been properly licensed and that they had spoken no additions to the licensed text, they were given a 'sharp and sound reproof' and banned from playing until further notice. The King's anger cooled quickly, however, and some ten days later a letter from the Earl of Pembroke to the President of the Council conveyed the King's wish that since their punishment 'stops the current of their poor livelihood' the actors should be allowed to recommence playing, on condition that they would never again perform *A Game at Chess*. Although summoned too, Middleton failed to appear and a warrant to apprehend him was issued. Unable to find the author, the authorities arrested his son, Edward, but he could offer no useful information and was released. There the matter seems to have rested, and a story that

Middleton was imprisoned but obtained his release by writing
an apologetic poem to James is almost certainly apocryphal.


## VIII

Given the strict censorship, it may seem strange that the play
should have been licensed for performance in the first place. It
may be, however, that while the Master of the Revels (the
censor) was prepared to allow the attack on Catholicism and
satire on the Spanish match contained in the text, he could not
foresee the extensive detail the players would go to in their
portrayal of Gondomar. His task was to license play-texts not
productions, and it is not clear to what extent actual performances embellished those censored texts.

Penalties for contravening the censorship laws were harsh: in
1626, for example, a man was racked twice for writing a private
letter that included 'words and insinuations against His
Majesty', and Simonds D'Ewes kept his diary in code to avoid
detection (Hill, 1985; Clare, 1990). Even with a licence, therefore,
and despite the very large sums of money the company (who
raised their prices specially) seem to have made from the play
(even after paying the fines imposed by the Privy Council), the
risks involved in presenting A Game at Chess would have been
too great without the promise of protection from powerful men
close to the centre of government who were willing in the
circumstances to stir up the people.

A case has been made for the Duke of Buckingham as patron,
but not only is the play equivocal in its representation of the
White Duke, but there are other reasons why this seems
doubtful. Buckingham's wife had come from a Catholic family
and her 'conversion to the Church of England was most
superficial' (Willson, 1971: 427). More to the point, the play's
sharp anti-Jesuit stance may have caused Buckingham some
embarrassment, since his mother had been converted by the
Jesuit, Father Fisher, in 1622. Buckingham publicly disowned the
act, but privately petitioned James to allow Fisher to live under
his mother's protection. As a biographer has written, 'his
mother's conversion' was, in the end, 'singularly disastrous' for
Buckingham, 'since it provided a focus for all the latent

animosity against him' (Williamson, 1940: 112, 118–19). Some contemporaries also seem to have seen the play as derogatory to Buckingham. Writing in 1633, William Prynne inveighed against plays 'wherein sundry persons of place have been particularly personated, jeared, abused in a grosse and scurrilous manner', and cited as an example the attacks made in *A Game at Chess* on 'Gundemore' and 'the late Lord Admirall' – in other words, Buckingham.

Margot Heinemann suggests that while there is enough in the play of use to Buckingham to keep him neutral, there is more reason to see William Herbert, 3rd Earl of Pembroke – who was not only the Lord Chamberlain but the leader of the anti-Spanish group on the Privy Council – as the main figure behind the play. He was the personal patron of the King's Men, the Venetian ambassador termed him 'the head of the Puritans', and Gondomar himself referred to the Earl as the mortal enemy of Spain (Heinemann, 1982: 166–71). The Earl of Clarendon thought Pembroke was 'rather regarded and esteemed of King James than loved and favoured' and that he attracted the support 'of all who were displeased and unsatisfied in the court or with the court'. It is presumably not without significance that the censor, Sir Henry Herbert, was Pembroke's cousin, owed his advancement to the Earl, and did not lose his job as a result of the scandal.

Further support for the players undoubtedly came from the City. Middleton retained his post as Chronologer, though the 1624 Lord Mayor's Show was written by John Webster while Middleton was, presumably, maintaining a low profile. There was no mayoral pageant in 1625, but in 1626 Middleton was employed to provide another Lord Mayor's Show (*The Triumphs of Health and Prosperity*), while his widow was granted a pension after his death for the service he had done the City.

In 1605, Samuel Calvert observed that dramatists did not 'forbear to present upon their Stage the whole course of this present time', and *A Game at Chess*, like much of Middleton's other work, is evidence of his 'interventions' in contemporary issues. In other words, his play is not merely a reflection of opinions of the day, it is one of the means by which men and women formed those opinions; it is not to be set alongside the 'historical context' of 1623–4, but is itself part of that context, demonstrating, in Susan Sontag's words, that 'Art is not only about something; it is something. A work of art is a thing in the world, not just a text or commentary on the world' (1983: 142).

# 10
# Middleton: Summary and Conclusions

Thomas Middleton apparently began his solo writing career as a dramatist by writing *The Phoenix* for the Children of Paul's, a play possibly intended to restore that Company's reputation following the scandal over *The Old Joiner of Aldgate* (see Gair, 1982: ch. 5). In this play (now lost), George Chapman had put on the Paul's stage barely disguised representations of local men and women involved in vigorous legal wrangling over a marriage. It had been commissioned by one of those involved – a bookbinder named Flaskett whose business premises were in Paul's Yard – in an attempt to influence the court case in his favour. When it looked like the play might get him into trouble, however, Flaskett was able to argue that no commentary on affairs outside the theatre was intended, declaring that the play was 'onely a meere Toye which had idle applications of names according to the Inventors disposicion thereof', even though the play's success resulted precisely from the audience being able to identify the protagonists. It seems appropriate, therefore, that Middleton should conclude his playwriting career by producing a scandal on the grand scale, representing characters playing out their parts not in the neighbourhood of St Paul's Cathedral, but on the world stage.

Although his plays were evidently popular, Middleton himself does not appear to have been particularly praised in his

140

own time. Ben Jonson, for example (who succeeded Middleton as Chronologer of the City of London), called him 'but a base fellow' and suggested that Gondomar used *A Game at Chess* for 'cleansing his posterior', while William Hemminge described him as 'squoblinge' [quarrelsome], and adored only by Puritans on their way to hell. Both these views seem to take exception more to Middleton's manner and beliefs than to his skill, however, and so it may be unsurprising that one of the few commendations of Middleton's work was written by a Puritan, Nathaniel Richards, himself the author of a number of anti-Jesuit satires. In a verse prefacing the 1657 edition of *Women Beware Women*, Richards calls Middleton 'amongst the best/Of poets in his time', and the printer of the edition claimed that 'those issues of his brain that have already seen the sun have by their worth gained themselves a free entertainment amongst all that are ingenious.'

In recent times Middleton's reputation has gradually grown, particularly in the theatre, though there it is still on the basis of a fairly small selection of his output, and it would be good to see some of the less well-known, yet remarkable, plays, such as *The Witch* and *A Mad World, My Masters*, performed on the professional stage.

Although it may often, in Arthur Symons words, 'shine like fire and cut like ice', Middleton's writing is notable for the plainness of its style; the analogy he draws in the Preface to *The Roaring Girl* between his language and the simple, straightforward dress then in fashion is applicable to his work overall. Middleton does, however, create frameworks of key words (the use of 'service' in *The Changeling*, or 'stranger' and 'peace' in *Women Beware Women*, for example), and of images (such as those of 'sight' and 'blindness' in *The Changeling* and *A Mad World, My Masters*), to sustain the plays' governing ideas.[1]

Matched with this is his ability to create a complex structure of often contradictory modes and forms, a brilliant touch in linking, or contrasting, verbal language with startling stage images, and a keen understanding of the fundamental metaphor provided by the theatrical performance itself.

The sharp irony in language and action that pervades, even characterises, Middleton's work, has at times been seen as indicative of a coolly detached approach to his subject matter. In an essay praising Middleton, T. S. Eliot wrote famously (but misleadingly) that he 'has no point of view, is neither sentimental nor cynical; he is neither resigned, nor disillusioned, nor romantic, he has no message' (1963: 84), and in a generally unfavourable essay L. C. Knights complained that (certainly in his comedies) Middleton's work was not 'unified by a dominant attitude' (1962: 223). More recently, John McElroy[2] has argued that Middleton's early comedy is intended solely to entertain and 'leaves little for the intellect to ponder and still less for the conscience to feed upon'. For me, however, what emerges from Middleton's work is a sense of passion and intellect combined, a consistent view of the world that is shaped by his religious and political beliefs and finds expression in his engagement in the major issues of his time. The fact that he frequently employs theatrical strategies that allow an audience to maintain a critical attitude to characters and events (in which some modern critics have suggested similarities with Brecht's dramaturgy) should in no way diminish our sense of the strength of his commitment to the ideas themselves.[3]

Let an anonymous seventeenth-century fan have the final word:

> Facetious Middleton, thy witty Muse
> Hath pleased all that books or men peruse.
> If any thee despise, he doth but show
> Antipathy to wit in daring so.
> Thy fame's above his malice and 'twill be
> Dispraise enough for him to censure thee.[4]

# 11
# 'The Revenger's Tragedy'

I

As its title and the name of its central character advertise, *The Revenger's Tragedy* (1606) clearly belongs to the genre of Revenge Tragedy (see chapter 12). Other roots, dramatic and non-dramatic, can also be identified, mainly the Morality play, the homilies of medieval preachers, contemporary Jacobean satire, as well as various iconographic traditions. The influence of all of these can be found in the opening speech which, in terms of its staging, form and content, demonstrates many of the stylistic approaches and theatrical strategies of the play as a whole.[1]

The opening presents the audience with the first of the play's many striking stage images, as Vindice, holding a skull, observes a procession of figures 'pass over the stage with torchlight'. Vindice is placed, as it were, with one foot in the play-world, and one in the world of the audience, a position that shifts within this speech and throughout the play. He begins with a commentary on the procession:

> Duke: royal lecher; go, grey haired Adultery,
> And thou his son, as impious steeped as he:
> And thou his bastard true begot in evil:

And thou his duchess that will do with devil:
For ex'lent characters.

(I. i. 1–5)[2]

Vindice's first role resembles that of the Morality play presenter, but in his use of the word 'character' he shades into that of the contemporary satirist. The word 'character' was not used in the Jacobean period to refer to people in plays (it did not acquire this meaning until the eighteenth century), but to short 'character sketches' of contemporary types. Sir John Overbury, who published a popular collection in 1615, described a 'Character' as 'a picture . . . quaintly drawn in various colours, all of them heightened by one shadowing'. This manner of exaggerated, selective representation, and the naming of the characters to identify their particular qualities (Castiza–Chastity, Lussurioso–Lechery, and so on), each commented on by an acerbic observer, indicates the play's fusion of the Morality tradition with contemporary satiric comedy such as that written by Middleton, Marston and Jonson. It is a conjunction that provides a guide to the kind of play this is – closer to satiric comedy than to tragedy – in which 'a deliberately stylised and mannered technique was fundamentally necessary' (New Mermaids edition: xvi).

As Vindice gets into his stride he admonishes the audience, using the skull as a *memento mori* in the manner of the medieval preacher. This section of the speech (9–38), in which he praises Gloriana for refusing to consent to the Duke's 'palsey-lust' (34), but rebukes women in general for their face painting – their 'bought' complexions – reveals the dichotomy in Vindice between admiration and misogynous mistrust that informs his behaviour to his sister and mother later in the play and prompts his use of Gloriana's skull, dressed in finery and painted with cosmetics, as an accessory in the murder of the Duke (III. v).

In the third section of the speech (39–44) Vindice addresses neither the audience nor the skull: 'here Revenge speaks to Vengeance' (Mooney, 1983: 167–8), revealing Vindice's awareness not only of his role as an individual within the play, but also of the 'quality' he represents, indicated by the character's name. Vindice plays on this self-awareness constantly, calling the audience's attention to the fact that they are watching a play, to the particular kind of play they are watching, and to the conventional expectations of the roles he plays within it.

At the close of the speech, Vindice re-establishes contact first with the skull and then with the audience before Hippolito enters and he moves into the on-stage world of the play (44–9).

## II

The self-conscious theatricality revealed in the opening speech is enforced throughout the play at the level of language and action. Vindice 'writes' scenes for himself and 'directs' others (such as II. i, III. v, V. i), occasionally bursting into delighted applause at his own inventiveness. Other characters, too, construct experiences in theatrical terms – Junior's execution, for example, 'is imagined in terms of a scaffold [another term for a stage] and "gaping people"' (III. iii. 20) (Wharton, 1988: 49), and 'revels' (with the masque at their centre) are the time when most villainy is enacted. Vindice also takes on different parts, each of which reveals another facet of his nature; indeed, the two key roles he adopts – Court Bawd and disaffected Melancholic – may be construed as twin poles of his personality.

## III

The contrast of tones, attitudes and styles in Vindice's opening soliloquy (desire/repulsion, irony/passionate engagement, pronouncements on the terror of death undercut with jokes) contributes to the play's dominant impression of contradiction. As Brian Gibbons observes of the opening scene (New Mermaids: xx–xxi)

It begins in meditative stillness; the entry of a character initiates the planning of an intrigue and provokes a display of satiric wit, and the entry of further characters brings mounting complexity and speed to the action and a prevalent tone of un-sentimental, curbed cynicism and precarious, sardonic comedy.

Similar patterns may also be found in sequences of scenes. Following the opening scene, for example, the play moves speedily from the sharp satire of the corrupt court (I. ii) to the brooding verse of the Duchess's attempt to seduce Spurio, which in turn moves to Spurio (building on the relationship with the audience he has established earlier in the scene) informing the audience directly, almost conversationally, of his origins and proposed vengeance. The rapid verbal jokes of I. iii between Vindice and Lussurioso, many made directly to the audience, differ sharply from the tone and method of I. iv, where there are no asides or passages of direct address. Indeed, after the sheer energy of the preceding action it is the stillness of the scene that effects the strongest contrast. The tableau presented – Antonio's wife, who has committed suicide in shame after being raped by Junior, lying with a 'prayer book the pillow to her cheek' (14), and another 'Placed in her right hand with a leaf tucked up,/Pointing to these words:/*Melius virtute mori, quam per dedecus vivere*' (16–18: 'Better to die in virtue than live in dishonour') – is an image reminiscent of the emblematic woodcuts popular at the time, and a further instance of the playwright's awareness of the power of stage images.[3]

As these examples illustrate, it is clearly part of the playwright's conscious strategy to move rapidly, at times disorientingly, through a variety of moods and styles, and this is reflected too in the way the writing shifts, often with startling suddenness, from witty and acerbic prose, laden with sexual innuendo, to verse described by Swinburne (1887: 5) as having a 'cadence which . . . utters the cry of an anguish too deep for weeping'.


IV


As the play develops, and the various intrigues set up in the first act begin to spawn other revenges and to helter-skelter into scenes of increasing violence, it becomes equally clear that the dramatist is particularly concerned to set that violence in a comic – at times even farcical – context of language and action, to maintain an equal tension between the two, and so suspend the audience uneasily, yet thrillingly, between laughter and shock.

In II. ii, for example, Vindice (disguised as Piato, a name that means 'hidden') incites Lussurioso with the information (which Vindice believes accurate) that his stepmother is even at that moment in bed with her bastard stepson, Spurio. Beside himself with fury, Lussurioso plunges into the bedroom (II. iii) to be confronted by his stepmother in bed – but with the Duke. On one level this is the stuff of farce, and should be played as such (that is, completely seriously) with the audience, themselves surprised, able to enjoy the various levels of astonishment and discomfort of the characters – including Vindice. At the same time there is a serious undercurrent to the moment since the danger is real, and Lussurioso's sole comment ('I am amazed to death' – l. 14) 'has a deeper meaning than he suspects, as he is shortly taken off to be sentenced'. Only by allowing both the comic and serious strands to coexist equally strongly will a production impress itself in the theatre as a 'disturbing and serious play' (Foakes, 1978: 62).

At other times the audience is provided with prior information that enables them to view the confusion with a detached and ironical eye, such as when Supervacuo's and Ambitioso's glee at obtaining what they believe to be the severed head of Lussurioso is confounded first by his appearance, and, after his exit, by their discovery of the true contents of the bag – the head of their younger brother, Junior, whose safe release they intended. Only in performance, really, can the potency of the juxtaposition of the 'bleeding head' and the comedy of Supervacuo's threat to the Officer ('I'll brain thee with it' – III. vi. 77) be properly enjoyed.

Without doubt, the most complex scene in the play (and one that certainly cannot be fully experienced outside performance) is act III, scene v, the scene of the Duke's murder, which draws together most of the points made so far. The scene opens with Vindice introducing the audience to the 'property' of the skull of Gloriana, his dead lover, dressed in her clothes. It is important that Vindice initially conceals from the audience the fact that it is not a real woman (not difficult for the actor to do), so that their response (shared by Hippolito) is one of shock and surprise – no doubt mixed with a macabre fascination: the worlds of the

Grotesque and the Gothic Horror are close. The dual perspective – a skull dressed in fine clothes – that Vindice challenges the audience to confront, is further enforced by the dislocation of image and language as Vindice moves from some of the most powerful verse in the play (the celebrated silkworm speech) and begins to tell black jokes, referring to his companion as 'the boney lady', who is 'a little/Bashful at first as most of them are, but after/The first kiss the worst is past with them' even though 'She's somewhat/A grave look with her'. If the audience remembers his earlier claims for Gloriana's virtue, this prostitution of her remains will further complicate their responses to Vindice and his actions.

Almost gently, shyly, the Duke approaches for the kiss, and as his lips touch the skull the pace and rhythm of the scene shifts up a gear. As the Duke's lips start to be eaten away by the poison, Vindice and Hippolito tell more jokes, the cruelty and humour underlined by the elegance of the shared lines, the disjunction for the audience being contained in the contrast of their language with, strictly speaking, the Duke's noise, as he screams in agony.

DUKE:  My teeth are eaten out!
VINDICE:    Hadst any left?
HIPPOLITO:    I think but few.
VINDICE:  Then those that didst eat are eaten.  (159–60)

More complex still is the image with which the scene concludes as the Duke, his tongue 'nailed down' and his eyelids torn up, is forced to watch another 'play' as his wife embraces his bastard son. In the background, as the scent of the perfume wafts in the air, the happy music of the revels is heard. At this moment, and contained within the same 'frame', virtually all the audience's senses are simultaneously employed and brought into collision with each other.

It is perhaps not surprising that a theatrical strategy such as one finds in this scene and throughout the play has attracted criticism: William Archer, for instance, described the author as a 'sanguinary maniac' with a 'gloating appetite for horrors'.[4] But in presenting these contrasts and conflicts – in the play's structure, within individual characters and in the language – the playwright is clearly attempting not merely to describe, but to embody in the form of the play the sense of a shifting and chaotic world, an aim he shares with other contemporary playwrights and writers. In its formal qualities, the play also shares many of the stylistic characteristics of contemporary Mannerist painting. There too one finds radical juxtapositions in form, and frequently too a figure who stands, looking out from the picture to the viewer, bridging the gap between the worlds of each, just as Vindice does in the play. It should be stressed, however, that Mannerism and the Grotesque (as the approach is usually referred to in literature), are not mere playing with form, but are attempts to reproduce experiences of fracture and collision and uncertainty. As Cyrus Hoy has written:

> It would be odd if so thorough-going a revolution in man's conception of himself, his world, and his relation to deity – all accomplished within the limits of a single century – had not left its impact on the art of the sixteenth and seventeenth centuries and of course it has done so, both on the art of literature, and on the arts of painting, architecture and sculpture.[5]

It is precisely this tension – in this play most commonly between laughter and horror; Nicholas Brooke's phrase 'horrid laughter' is a good one – that distinguishes the Grotesque from its near-neighbour, tragicomedy, in which the mood is ultimately optimistic and where endings aim to create a mood of harmonious re-establishment of order and reconciliation (see chapter 6). Furthermore, in tragicomedies the modes and moods are distinct rather than fused, allowing the audience to move from one to the other, whereas the disorientating effect of the Grotesque is caused by the speed with which the contrasts are experienced, requiring actors – and audience – to turn on a sixpence. It is inevitable that to collate such a response through reading alone will prove extremely difficult, but even in the theatre, the only place where the full effect can be achieved, resistance can be strong.

When *The Revenger's Tragedy* was revived in 1966 by the Royal Shakespeare Company at Stratford, the production (directed by Trevor Nunn) was criticised unfavourably by a number of press reviewers for emphasising the comic, at times farcical, elements in the text as strongly as the more serious ones, in an overall production style that sought to give due attention to the play's discordant tone. The *Sunday Telegraph* reviewer, for example, wrote:

> One of the most vicious, perverse and evil tragedies in English drama is now clogged with buffoonery. . . . the Royal Shakespeare Company has allowed horror to be crazy-ganged into stupidness, dissipating the intensity of the drama so that the situations lose their chill.

This view appears to stem from the belief that a comic view of the world is somehow less valid or momentous than a tragic, and accordingly privileges one mode above another. It therefore misses the key point, which is that the 'jest' (or the 'game') is not merely a pale imitation of the 'earnest' or reality – in fact, as examples from *Women Beware Women* and *A Fair Quarrel* demonstrated, it may be a truer, harder version of the 'reality'. As Keith Thomas (1977: 77) has written in an essay on laughter in the Elizabethan and Jacobean periods: 'Jokes are a pointer to joking situations, areas of structural ambiguity in society itself; and their subject matter can be a revealing guide to past tensions and anxieties.'

## V

The play is set in Italy. In part, the use of foreign locations or historical periods (such as Middleton employed in *Women Beware Women* and *Hengist*) provided a smokescreen behind which a writer could operate, hoping to avoid the censorship regulations. Italy, however, carried particular resonance for a Jacobean audience, who considered it the home and source of every kind of depravity. Thomas Nashe's description in *The Unfortunate Traveller* (1594) is typical:

> Italy, the paradise of the earth and the epicure's heaven, how doth it form our young master? . . . From thence he brings the

art of atheism, the art of epicurising, the art of whoring, the
art of poisoning, the art of sodomitry. . . . It is now a privy
note amongst the better sort of men, when they would set a
singular brand on a notorious villain, to say he hath been in
Italy.[6]

As J. W. Lever stresses, however, this view of Italy was based on
facts 'which make the inventions of the Jacobeans rather pedes-
trian' (he quotes some startling examples), so that 'the basis of
truth underlying a stylized approach added to the play's
validity' (Lever, 1987: 19–20). Clearly, though, the contemporary
audience would have readily perceived in the play a satirical
commentary on the notorious decadence of the English court,
and on London 'society'. In *Laugh and Lie Downe: Or, the Worldes
Folly*, one C. T. (who might have been Cyril Tourneur) wrote of
London and its inhabitants in a tone very similar to that of the
play:

> Now in this Town were many sundry sorts of people of all
> ages; as old and young and middle age: men, women and
> children: which did eat, and drink, and make a noise, and
> die . . . they were creatures that served the time, followed
> shadows, fitted humours, hoped of fortune, and found, what?
> I cannot tell you.  (quoted in Dollimore, 1984: 144)

This critique of court life, its decadence contrasted with the
innocence and honesty of the country, provides a further serious
dimension to the play that is set against its comic elements to
create still more tension. Phrases such as 'this present minute',
'our present age', 'this luxurious day wherein we breathe', 'This
night, this hour, this minute – now' run through the play,
stressing the present tense; it is a play of immediacy, as events
occur with startling suddenness, taking the audience, as well as
the characters themselves, by surprise. The sense conveyed by
the language and rhythms of the play of characters being driven
for instant gratification of their obsessive desires ('hurry, hurry,
hurry' – II. i. 202) is matched by an equal stress on the
inexorable march of death and decay, the physical nature of the
world being enforced through a network of images of the body

and food, of sex and sexual desire, and of change.[7] As Castiza says:

> The world's so changed one shape into another,
> It is a wise child now that knows her mother.
>                         (II. i. 161–2)

The play also makes reference to a range of social problems. The opening scene sets Vindice's personal misery against a wider framework with references to land ownership and loss. The 'discontent' of which his father died no doubt refers to the economic ruin that followed a fall from favour at court, and in disguise as Piato, Vindice bases his temptation of Castiza (II. i) on a catalogue of social ills and the sheer folly of exchanging chastity for poverty. The ease with which Vindice tempts his mother with promise of escape from their straitened circumstances, and her references to 'mean people, ignorant people' as she aligns herself with 'the better sort' (II. i. 145–6), reveal the social effects of the court, just as Vindice in his 'malcontent' role (IV. ii) sets out the miseries of going to law and the ruin it brings.

Much of the direct and topical social criticism in Vindice's discourse may – understandably – be cut in performance since it can prove obscure to a modern audience, but this omission has the effect of removing one of the ways by which the playwright shifts the audience's perception of Vindice and his motivation. At the opening of the play, Vindice is presented to some extent as a positive figure. He is a man set aside from society, a man not only with a 'just' reason for revenge (the deaths of his lover and father both result from the Duke's actions), but also a scourge of the corruption and depravity of the court. As such, it is likely that he would attract the audience's sympathy, helped by and reflected in his direct interaction with them, verbally and physically.

As the play progresses, however, the balance in Vindice between fascination and disgust, 'justice' and 'vengeance', satiric presenter and self-deceiver, that the opening speech hinted at, shifts. The susceptibility to corruption that is clearly in him from the start of the play (he praises Gloriana's beauty above her virtue, for example) emerges ever more strongly. The disguises he adopts allow him to pursue his intrigues, but the ease with which he adopts them also suggests his affinity with the court: at one point he is hired to kill himself, which neatly catches his double nature, and in the masque at the end he is indistinguishable from the other murderers. His decision to pursue the temptation of his sister and mother, and the passion with which he articulates the sensual pleasures of the court, seem to reveal deeper desires within him, and the professed virtue of Vindice and Hippolito in the 'scourging' of their mother is mediated by the damning parallels the play draws between them and Ambitioso and Supervacuo.

The turning point comes at the end of III. v. Strictly speaking, Vindice's vengeance should be concluded with the murder of the Duke. His decision to proceed ('As fast as they peep up, let's cut 'em down' – III. v. 219), especially when innocent bystanders start to get killed, moves him further into the world of the play, reflected in the fact that from this point his direct interaction with the audience is severely reduced.[8] He still continues to use such bridging terms as 'we', 'us' and so on, but the audience may well now resist such implicating speech acts. In the end, all that distinguishes Vindice from the other revengers is his superior skill and wit, the quaintness of his malice, rather than the justice (however wild) of his actions. The roles he first adopted – of Moralist, Satirist, and Revenger – have either been discarded or distorted: now killing, or more exactly the pleasure of killing, is everything.

## VI

A masque is treason's licence, that build upon –
'Tis murder's best face, when a vizard's on
                              (V. i. 176–7)

As in many Elizabethan and Jacobean plays, the climax comes in the form of a masque, the revels after a banquet.[9] It is an appropriate ending thematically for a play of disguise and deception and draws to a close the image of the Dance of Death that threads through the play, as Lussurioso, installed as Duke and 'ready now for sports', promises:

> Ah, 'tis well,
> Brothers and bastard, you dance next in hell!
> $\qquad$ (V. iii. 38, 40–1)

The final masque completes a pattern that began even before the play's action started. Spurio was conceived, he tells us:

> After some gluttonous dinner – some stirring dish
> Was my first father; when deep healths went round
> And ladies cheeks were painted red with wine
> $\qquad$ (I. ii. 179–81)

and Antonio recalls that:

> $\qquad$ last revelling night,
> When torchlight made an artificial noon
> About the court, some courtiers in the mask

raped his wife:

> When music was heard loudest, courtiers busiest,
> And ladies great with laughter – Oh vicious minute!
> $\qquad$ (I. iv. 27–9, 39–40)

The Duke's murder, in an 'unsunned lodge/Wherein 'tis night at noon' (III. v. 18–19), is also played out against a background of off-stage music and feasting. The events surrounding the final 'murder in a masque' are deliberately chaotic and intentionally comic: in this it prefigures the more complex chaos of Middleton's elaborate finale to *Women Beware Women*, and as in the later play, though these people's lives and values are dangerous, they are also ridiculous, and there should be no attempt in performance to control or stifle an audience's desire to laugh.


### VII

It is not perhaps surprising that a play which seeks constantly to set up contrasts and contradictions in its action and audience response should attract equally contradictory interpretations of its ultimate intentions.

At the close of the play, despite his earlier denial that he would do so (V. i. 87–90, 152), Vindice 'unmasks' and confesses all, only to be condemned to death. This has been seen by some critics as the last in the series of brilliant ironical reversals that run throughout the play, but which, this time, demonstrates the intervention of some greater power (in the form of Providence), confirms the play's statement on the futility of trying to conceal the truth from 'that eternal eye/That sees through flesh and all' (I. iii. 66–7), and results in establishing a 'good' ruler on the throne (Lisca, 1959). Belief in providential interventions was current and strong: an engraving of 1605, for example, shows Guy Fawkes entering Parliament under cover of darkness, but illuminated by a ray of light beaming down from an eye set in the sky above, an inscription in the beam reading 'Caelitus discussa' – 'Overthrown by heavenly aid'.

Other critics, however, believe that the play challenges rather than promotes such a traditional, conservative view. They argue that throughout the final act the conventional sign of God's presence (thunder) has been mocked, transformed to a stage effect (V. ii. 42), and that the 'blazing star' that rises, a traditional device of medieval drama was, by 1606, perceived as old-fashioned: as Alexander Leggatt (1988: 123) observes, the 'sceptical gaze of Jacobean drama is also trained on the heavens'.

I suspect the play is intended to resist either clear-cut interpretation. As I suggested above, the action of the play is clearly intended to shift our perception of, and attitude to, Vindice by the close, portraying him as a character (like Beatrice-Joanna in *The Changeling*) whose corruption is at first not apparent but which emerges as the action develops. At the same time, however, I do not find a sense of harmony and order  being restored, or established, through the death of Vindice and accession of Antonio.

Antonio's first action as ruler is, after all, like Lussurioso's before him, to order an execution without trial. Indeed, Antonio perhaps proves a more skilful – and secret – Machiavel than anyone, rather than the presager of 'the silver age again,/When there was fewer but more honest men' (V. iii. 86–7): there are certainly fewer men around than at the start of the play, but just how 'honest' they are is unclear.

The playwright's apparent refusal to offer a fully resolved closure is reflected in his determination to maintain to the end a challenging mix of styles. The farcical denouement of the masque is followed first by Antonio's brusque instructions for Vindice's and Hippolito's deaths, and then by Vindice's sardonic, even light-hearted acceptance of his fate:

> And now my lord, since we are in for ever
> This work was ours, which else might have been slipped;
> And if we list we could have nobles clipped
> And go for less than beggars. But we hate
> To bleed so cowardly: we have enough –
> I'faith we're well – our mother turned, our sister true,
> We die after a nest of dukes! Adieu.
>
> (V. iii 120–6)

Even the uncertainty of Antonio's closing line, 'Pray heaven their blood may wash away all treason' (129) leaves the play and its audience in a precarious state. As Jonathan Dollimore (1988: 148) observes, however, 'Given a world of dislocated energy as its dramatic subject, what kind of formal unity is such a play likely to possess?' It is evident that, far from being a simple *tour de force* of theatrical pyrotechnics, the play presents a vision – and a critique – of a world gone crazy, and embodies the experience of such chaos and confusion through its impact on the audience and in its refusal to reconcile this discord in a conveniently clear-cut closure.

One study of the Grotesque notes that: 'It is no accident that the grotesque mode in art and literature tends to be prevalent in societies and eras marked by strife, radical change or disorientation.'[10] The writer is here referring to the twentieth century, but what he says may be applied equally to Jacobean society. It may help us to understand more fully the desire of dramatists such as Middleton (and if he *is* someone else, the author of *The Revenger's Tragedy*), to 'poison in jest'.[11]

# 12

# 'The Atheist's Tragedy or The Honest Man's Revenge'

I

Very little is known of the life of Cyril Tourneur. He was born sometime between 1570 and 1580, after which virtually no record of him exists until 1614, when he is referred to in a letter as 'one Cyril Turner, that belongs to General Cecil and was in former times Secretary to Sir Francis Vere'. Cecil took Tourneur with him as Secretary of the Council of War when he sailed to raid Spanish treasure ships in Cadiz in 1625. The expedition was a failure and when, on the voyage home, plague broke out on board the flagship *Royal Anne*, Tourneur was one of 150 sick men put ashore at Kinsale in Ireland. He died there in February 1626.

As Peter B. Murray has written, this anonymity, added to the the emphasis given to the question of the authorship of *The Revenger's Tragedy* (Murray thinks it is Middleton's) has 'so greatly affected most critics that they have been able to see Tourneur's other works only as leading up to or away from it' (Murray, 1964: 7). Leaving aside *The Revenger's Tragedy*, these other works consist of just five poems, two plays (one of which has been lost) and part of another (though there is no record of whether it was ever finished or produced), and a pamphlet. Of these items, five cannot be attributed with certainty to Tourneur and without them the available material on which to base arguments for ascribing *The Revenger's Tragedy* is very meagre indeed (see Appendix I).

There is, however, no doubt about the authorship of *The Atheist's Tragedy*. It was printed in 1611 with the title-page naming Cyril Tourneur as the author and indicating that 'in diuers places it hath often beene Acted'. We do not know to which theatres this refers, and therefore cannot make specific use of the quite detailed staging information, implicit and explicit, that the text gives. The play requires the use of two doors, a pit (used for the charnel house in IV. iii), an arras, and V. iii seems to indicate the use of an upper level and a raised platform for the scaffold.

## II

*The Atheist's Tragedy* has been described as a 'thesis' play, and more specifically as 'an explicit dramatical projection of the themes of the 127th Psalm, "*Nisi Dominus*, nothing can be done without God's grace"', neither of which makes the play sound particularly appealing.[1] Indeed, any reader or audience coming new to the play might understandably be deterred by the first scene. Understandably, but mistakenly, since the opening – which aims to establish the basis of the argument as clearly as possible 'without the intrusion of narrative or emotion' (New Mermaids edition 1974: xi; all line references are to this edition) – is followed by a play that offers a totally new perspective on the subject of revenge, presented in a startling variety of styles and moods.

The play's basic structure is straightforward. It sets up two opposing viewpoints (each represented by a character), and proceeds to trace the arguments and demonstrate the events that prove one superior to the other. D'Amville, the atheist, argues that there is nothing beyond Nature and that essentially nothing distinguishes Man from the animals. D'Amville (it has been suggested that his name approximates 'damned villain') is

absolute in his evil. He sums up his philosophy as being
'pleasure or profit' (IV. iii. 112–13), and his actions in the pursuit
of the satisfaction of these appetites (the disinheritance of
Charlemont, the murder of Montferrers, the forced marriage of
Castabella to Rousard, and, ultimately, the attempt to rape
Castabella), and his linguistic frame of reference (images of
money, food and building predominate) reveal the secular and
temporal limits of his philosophy. In a sense, he may be
characterised through the couplet with which he concludes the
first scene:

> Let all men lose, so I increase my gain.
> I have no feeling of another's pain.
> (I. i. 128–9)

Although at the end of the play, confronted with the deaths of
his sons, D'Amville comes to recognise that:

> . . . Nature is a fool. There is a power
> Above her that hath overthrown the pride
> Of all my projects and posterity, . . .
> (V. ii. 258–60)

he remains essentially the same throughout, representing a fixed
idea; his knowledge is not gradually acquired but comes only in
the course of the last act. Like the traditional Vice figure of the
Morality plays with whom this character has affinities, there is
in his relentless evil and startling ability to play the honest man,
the kind of vitality that seduces an audience in much the same
way as can Quomodo or Richard III or Barabas (the Jew of
Malta).

The opposing argument is represented by his nephew, Charlemont, who is in every way the mirror-image of D'Amville: he is
the 'honest man', faithful and a soldier – the traditional opposite
of the counterfeiting politician. With a fortitude more Stoical
than Christian, Charlemont obeys (though not without a
struggle – see III. ii. 35–6, for example) the constraints laid upon
him, and entrusts his fate to the Providence that makes its
presence known through its thunderous and stellar inter-

ventions, but which is in this play not parodied and mocked as some suggest it is in *The Revenger's Tragedy* (see chapter 11).

*The Atheist's Tragedy's* rather straightforward main action is enriched and deepened by a number of smaller plot lines and characters that develop the presentation of the conflict between good and evil. Each main protagonist is matched by a female character, and just as D'Amville's atheism is thrown into contrast by Charlemont's faith, so Levedulcia's sexual depravity (incest, adultery) is shadowed by Castabella's chastity. These characters and plots not only give extra life to the central section of the play in which Charlemont is necessarily passive through imprisonment and his father's injunction, but offer more variety of characterisation than is possible with the more exemplary main characters. Sebastian and Rousard are contrasted as respectively vigorous and sickly, but both behave in unpredictable ways: Sebastian's response to Castabella's enforced marriage, or his attempt to help Charlemont, for example, when contrasted with his sexual relationship with Belforest's wife, make for a satisfyingly complex characterisation.[2]

However, while the play's basic ideas and its use of Morality techniques offer nothing innovatory or challenging, its treatment of the theme of revenge and its theatrical strategies certainly do.


### III


*'There is no heaven but Revenge'*
(Thomas Nashe, 1594)


The theme of revenge is prevalent in the drama of the late Elizabethan and early Jacobean period, and those plays in which it provides the mainspring of the action may be seen as a well-defined genre.[3] The basic model is Thomas Kyd's *The Spanish Tragedy* (c. 1589), though a combination of dramatic experiment and changing social attitudes to revenge resulted in a wide range of approaches as the period progressed.

Contemporary attitudes to revenge exhibit a tension between

the long-standing popular tradition of blood revenge for murder and the biblical and legal sanctions against it. The religious constraint may be summed up in the much quoted 'Vengeance is mine: I will repay, saith the Lord' (St Paul, Epistle to the Romans, XII: 19), the legal in a typical treatise – 'the law allowes or admittes no wager for bloud'. This tension was even more acute in the case of a son avenging his father, since 'There would be few Elizabethan's who would condemn the son's blood-revenge on a treacherous murderer whom the law could not apprehend for lack of proper legal evidence' (Bowers, 1966: 40), and Francis Bacon expressed something of the same idea in calling revenge a 'kind of wild justice'. The pull between these different viewpoints finds form in the drama in the shifting balance between the sympathy frequently shown by dramatists (and no doubt widely felt by audiences) towards the avenger-hero, and the conventional demand for his death at the end of the play.

What is unusual about *The Atheist's Tragedy*, however, is that it takes the basic components of the Kydian revenge play but creates a hero who fulfils in a central role the code of behaviour advanced by the moralists. It is the role enacted (if somewhat ambiguously) by Antonio in *The Revenger's Tragedy*, though there, until the closing scenes, the character is located at the edges of the play. It is a sign of the changing attitudes towards revenge that five years after *The Revenger's Tragedy* was performed, a character who shuns vengeance takes centre stage. This shift in approach in *The Atheist's Tragedy* is seen most clearly in the role given to the ghost, underlined by the clear distinction an audience would undoubtedly have drawn with the apparition in *Hamlet*. Consequently, Montferrers's command when he first appears to Charlemont must surely have contradicted the audience's expectation:

> Return to France, for thy old father's dead
> And thou by murder disinherited.
> Attend with patience the success of things,
> But leave revenge unto the King of kings.
> (II. vi. 19–22)

And later, unlike the ghost of King Hamlet who comes to chivvy along his hesitant son, Montferrers returns to *prevent* his son killing Sebastian:

> CHARLEMONT:
> Revenge, to thee I'll dedicate this work.
> MONTFERRERS:
> Hold, Charlemont!
> Let Him revenge my murder and thy wrongs
> To whom the justice of revenge belongs.
>
> (III. ii. 31–4)

These speeches identify Tourneur's decision to make *The Atheist's Tragedy* the first revenge play in which the hero is specifically forbidden to take revenge, as opposed to delaying through conscience, say, or some other constraint such as Amintor's discovery (in Beaumont and Fletcher's *The Maid's Tragedy*) that the man he has vowed to take vengeance on for cuckolding him is the king!

Charlemont nearly forgets himself in III. ii, but Tourneur has not taken what might have been the more interesting step dramatically of trying to explore the inner conflicts caused for the character by Montferrers's command, choosing instead to remove Charlemont to prison and so render the character almost constantly inactive. These innovations may result from a desire to tinker 'with the old machinery in order to produce a novel variation of an old theme which in essence was still popular' (Bowers, 1966: 143), or may reflect a changing attitude to revenge and its dramatic representation. Whatever the reason, the effect was considerable, and as *The Revenger's Tragedy* 'closes the first period in the history of Elizabethan revenge tragedy' (Bowers, 1966: 138), so *The Atheist's Tragedy* marks a major shift in the treatment of the theme in the drama overall. As the New Mermaids editors note (xxiv):

> The revenge theme was only available for a dramatist so long as no one wrote a play in which the Christian position was centrally adopted. Once Tourneur had written *The Atheist's Tragedy* there was nothing left for anyone to say on the

subject. Revenge plays, of a kind, continued to be written after 1611, but they went over and over the old ground.

IV

Here's a sweet comedy. 'T begins with *O Dolentis* and concludes with ha, ha, he. (II. iv. 84–5)

The structure of contrasted characters is carried into the fabric of the play. The most arresting feature of *The Atheist's Tragedy* is what Eliot (1963: 113) called its 'peculiar brew of styles', which ranges from an allegorical, emblematic mode in keeping with the play's Morality affinities, to a macabre, gothic humour, to a detailed 'domesticity' that has led one critic to (over?) state that 'the play offers as comprehensive and realistic a view of Jacobean daily life as any play of the period' (Revels edition: lvii).

The most striking example of the imaginative use of emblematic staging is the final moment when D'Amville executes himself (see below), but the most extensive is the description and discussion of the embroidery in IV. i, where the language (the whole section is one long *double entendre*), set against the simple domesticity of the artefact itself, is used to underline the depravity of the characters.[4]

The play makes extensive use of comedy, a blend of individual laugh lines and comic situations such as Fresco's desperate improvisation of the reason why he is in Levidulcia's bedroom (II. v). Striking contrasts of mood are also employed, which may arise from juxtaposed scenes (II. vi, III. i and III. ii, for example, with counterfeit and real ghosts), or within a single scene. Even though no scene in this play matches the extraordinary complexity of III. v in *The Revenger's Tragedy*, IV. iii comes close, with its mix of comedy and violence in language and action set against the symbolically powerful location of the charnel house within which it presents bizarre images such as the lovers lying each with 'a death's head for a pillow' (stage direction 205). For most of the scene the tones shift sequentially, though at certain moments (204–10, for example) they are presented virtually simultaneously, the ultimate goal of the Grotesque (see chapter 11).

V

Muriel Bradbrook (1966: 165) has written that Tourneur's plays are 'easy of interpretation on the surface', and in *The Atheist's Tragedy* the basic conflict – between Nature and God – and the ultimate moral – defy God and die – are clearly, to some critics, even 'bluntly' stated (New Mermaids: xxxvii). R. J. Kaufmann suggests that 'the premises of D'Amville's providential schemes make him seem more foolish than terrible' and he sees the self-execution (when D'Amville, in his haste to behead Charlemont, 'strikes out his own brains' with the axe – stage direction V. ii. 241) as 'a further example of the cosmic silliness of D'Amville's usurping role'.[5] This view is supported by Alan Dessen (1985: 112), who sees the moment as a kind of visual pun, 'a striking rebuttal to the claims and assumptions of this atheist who has relied solely upon his reason or "brains".'

Others have argued that the play's target may possibly be more specific than the general portrayal of the struggle between good and evil, and have suggested that it represents a conservative thinker's concern about the new science, the sceptical thinking that seemed in John Donne's words 'to call all in doubt'. When the ghost of the murdered Montferrers appears to D'Amville, for example, he immediately explains the apparition along the lines of contemporary thinking. Indeed, Charlemont initially does likewise when the ghost visits him, but almost immediately he reverts to a traditional theological and spiritual line of argument.

Finally, another interpretation is offered by Jonathan Dollimore who, while he acknowledges that the play is ostensibly 'a piece of unmitigated propaganda for a retributive providentialism' suggests that the ludicrous manner of D'Amville's death 'which hilariously parodies the by then rather tired dramatic convention whereby divine punishment is not only done but seen to be done' may possibly be intended to question 'the tragic didactic status of providentialism' (Dollimore, 1984: 88–9).

On the whole, the play has not fared well at the hands of critics, largely through the constant comparisons made with *The Revenger's Tragedy*, and, even though I suspect it may work well in performance, it has virtually no history of production on the professional stage against which to test the various critical responses; a production at the Belgrade Theatre, Coventry, in 1979, appears to be the only one.[6] In many ways, the view of an anonymous contemporary sums up the most common attitude to Tourneur:

> His fame unto that pitch so only raised
> As not to be despised nor too much praised.[7]

# Appendix I
## 'The Revenger's Tragedy':
## Middleton's or Tourneur's?

### I

To my knowledge, only one edition of *The Revenger's Tragedy* attributes the play to Middleton rather than Tourneur, and even then the editors express some reservations (Loughrey and Taylor, *Thomas Middleton: Five Plays*, 1988; see below). Of the two writers, however, the case for Middleton, if not conclusive, is by far the stronger.

On 7 October 1607, the printer George Eld submitted 'Twoo plaies' to the censor, Sir George Buc, for licensing – 'th[e] one called the revengers tragedie th[e] other A trick to catche the old one'. *The Revenger's Tragedy* had probably been written and performed the previous year. When it was published, the title page of the quarto carried no author's name (not unusual for the period), but noted that the play 'hath beene sundry times Acted, by the Kings Maiesties Seruants' (at the Globe). With no name indicated in either instance there is, on the face of it, no external evidence to support a claim for any particular author.

Other factors, however, point forcefully towards Middleton as the playwright. David Lake has noted that 'there is no instance of the coupling of plays known to be by different authors through the entire Elizabethan and Jacobean periods', while 'there are several couplings of plays by the same author' (Lake, 1975: 140). Middleton is the undisputed author of *A Trick* and Lake concludes that 'if *The Revenger's Tragedy* is not by the same author as *A Trick to Catch the Old One*, then it is *the sole exception to this rule* in the reigns of Elizabeth and James' (Lake, 1975: 141; my emphasis).

In his commendatory verse attached to the printed text of *Women Beware Women* (another undisputed Middleton play), Nathaniel Richards used the phrase 'drabs of state' (l. 2). This is a quotation from *The Revenger's Tragedy*, a fact that must have been known to Richards, since he used the complete line ('A drab of state, a cloth of silver slut') in his own play, *Messalina*, and other references in the verses indicate that Richards was well acquainted with Middleton and his work. The inclusion of these words from *The Revenger's Tragedy* in a tribute to Middleton may well suggest some link between the two.

At the time *The Revenger's Tragedy* was produced, Middleton's extant, undisputed work, appears to have been written solely for the boys' companies, most notably the series of satiric, city comedies for the Children of Paul's. Some critics have consequently considered it unlikely that in this situation Middleton would have written a 'tragedy' for the adult King's Men. But Middleton had already been employed by an adult company (Henslowe's Admiral's – later Prince's – Men) for whom he had written one tragedy (now lost) called *Randall, Earl of Chester*, and collaborated on another, and it has been suggested that he had already worked for the King's Men, collaborating with Shakespeare on *Timon of Athens*.

It has also been suggested that *The Revenger's Tragedy* might have been written with performance by a boys' company in mind, and then acquired later in some way by the King's Men when the Children of Paul's company folded, as it appears they did in 1606. This theory is supported by the play's use of the mannered technique typical of the work performed by the boy actors in the private theatres, and by the fact that in May 1606 Middleton provided *The Viper and Her Brood* (now lost) for the Children of the Queen's Revels. It has at times been proposed that this was *The Revenger's Tragedy* under another name, but whether that is so or not, the play appears to show Middleton writing a tragedy (it certainly does not sound like the title of a comedy) for a private theatre at the right date. Peter Thomson's observation (1983: 77) that *The Revenger's Tragedy* was not particularly successful in its own time indicates, perhaps, that the Globe audience was unready for the play's particular strategies.

In many ways the effort to demonstrate that Middleton might have produced a tragedy in 1606 is fruitless, since *The Revenger's Tragedy* is arguably more akin to the city comedies than to conventional tragedy, a cross-over noted by Brian Gibbons (1980: 121) when he writes that in Middleton's satirical comedy *Michaelmas Term* 'the dark and savage potential of the action expresses itself with a power more usually found in satiric tragedy', and, as Loughrey and Taylor (1988: xxvi) note, 'If one were worried that Middleton might have been moving too violently from comedy to tragedy in 1606–7, these observations might allay one's worries'.

Finally, it should be noted that many aspects of *The Revenger's Tragedy* – such as the bold mixture of comic and savage elements, the use of Morality play devices, the stance it takes on social issues, and the satirical view of court life it offers – though not unique to Middleton, are found not only in plays he is known to have written earlier, but remain characteristics of his outlook and dramatic method throughout his career.

## II

The attribution to Cyril Tourneur is, by comparison, very flimsy indeed, and anyone coming to it fresh may be surprised at the extent to which it has survived. Tourneur was first named as the author in a playlist published by Edward Archer in 1656 and attached as an appendix to a play also (ironically) involving Middleton – *The Old Law*, a tragicomedy, probably written in collaboration with his regular partner William Rowley, and (possibly) Philip Massinger. The attribution was repeated in subsequent lists issued in 1661 and 1671 by Francis Kirkman who, though he elaborated on the information, had no independent source: as usual he unquestioningly accepted Archer's (frequently totally wrong) ascriptions. Gerard Langbaine, again with no further evidence, repeated the attribution in 1691, which means that the ascription of the play to Tourneur is ultimately derived from Archer's original – and highly questionable – claim.

Towards the end of the nineteenth century scholars began to query the Tourneur attribution, but it was E. C. H. Oliphant who, in 1926, first made a specific claim for Middleton, since when others have joined in, supporting their arguments with a range of verbal, metrical, lexical and other stylistic analyses. Of these, the most detailed have been those of G. R. Price, M. P. Jackson, David Lake and P. B. Murray.[1]

Lake, even before he began his own study, considered that 'the conclusion must by now be almost irresistible that the copy for the substantive early quarto was a Middleton holograph' [a copy in the author's own handwriting] (Lake, 1975: 136). Following his own analysis Lake attributed 'every scene of *The Revenger's Tragedy* to Middleton: there is no convincing suggestion of any collaborator' (Lake, 1975: 142).

Others have been less convinced. R. A. Foakes, having edited the play for the Revels series, finds the evidence for Middleton's authorship 'strong but not conclusive', and on balance inclines towards Tourneur. Brian Gibbons, whose New Mermaids edition appeared in 1967, concludes that: 'it seems reasonable to ascribe the play to Cyril Tourneur, allowing that it reveals the influence of Thomas Middleton and John Marston and even, palely, like most Jacobean satiric plays, the influence of Ben Jonson' (xii).

Another editor, George Parfitt, considers that to attribute the play to either Tourneur or Middleton 'at the present state of play, would be irresponsible' and suggests that 'the play has to be regarded as anonymous.' He concludes:

It seems to me that we are not really even in a position to rule out the possibility that *The Revenger's Tragedy* is the work of a known dramatist other than Tourneur or Middleton, if we remember the versatility of most major Jacobean writers. (*The Plays of Cyril Tourneur*, Cambridge, 1978: xvii)

In 1966, Samuel Schoenbaum (who had earlier accepted Middleton's authorship, and included *The Revenger's Tragedy* in his critical study *Middleton's Tragedies*, 1955), offered his revised opinion:

the external evidence does not sweep all before it, and the situation, as it stands, is that neither Middleton's or Tourneur's advocates have been able to bring forward the kind of proof to which one party or the other must submit.[2]

Andrew Gurr, on the other hand, has taken the opposite course to Schoenbaum, and moved from rejection of Middleton in the first edition of *The Shakespearean Stage,* to acceptance in the second. Margot Heinemann's 'feeling that the play cannot confidently be taken as Middleton's is based on both dramatic and poetic style, as well as on the internal evidence', and she offers the view that while the author of *The Revenger's Tragedy* 'seems often to think in coloured images', Middleton's images, though visual, are, in the tragedies, limited to 'black and white, gold and silver' (Heinemann, 1982: 287–8).

The most recent contributions to the debate, however, have come down firmly on Middleton's side. *Thomas Middleton: Five Plays* includes *The Revenger's Tragedy*, providing, as the editors say, 'an opportunity to read *The Revenger's Tragedy* alongside some plays uncontroversially ascribed to Middleton', though even they admit that 'it would be dishonest of us to claim that our own subjective reading convinces us in the very marrow of our bones that *The Revenger's Tragedy* could only have come from the pen of Middleton' (Loughrey and Taylor, 1988: xxviii).

Roger Holdsworth (1990: 11), however, has no doubts on the matter: 'Thomas Middleton, and not Cyril Tourneur or anyone else, wrote *The Revenger's Tragedy*'. Apparently frustrated by the continued insistence on letting the absence of external evidence outweigh what he sees as the overwhelming internal (textual) evidence for Middleton's authorship, Holdsworth offers, in his essay, '*The Revenger's Tragedy* as a Middleton Play', an exhaustive analysis of the cross-references between Middleton's undisputed work – prose, poetry, masque and drama – up to and beyond *The Revenger's Tragedy*, to demonstrate how the play can be assimilated not only into Middleton's work up until 1606, but into the Middleton canon as a whole. He presents a vigorous and compelling case, and must surely advance still further the claim for Middleton to be accepted, at last, as the author of the play.

My own view, though more tentatively held than Roger

Holdsworth's, is that Middleton *is* the author, particularly in the light of David Lake's arguments, Anne Lancashire's analysis of the authorship of *The Second Maiden's Tragedy* and Roger Holdsworth's recent essay.[3]

But what of Cyril Tourneur, if *The Revenger's Tragedy* is not to be credited to him? Roger Holdsworth (1990: 13) suggests that as a result of Tourneur's name being linked with *The Revenger's Tragedy*, his undisputed play, *The Atheist's Tragedy*, 'instead of being as well known as *The Two Maids of Moreclack* or *The Duchess of Suffolk*, is widely studied and is currently in print in several paperback editions'. With comparatively few Elizabethan and Jacobean plays outside of Shakespeare's being studied and performed, I cannot think that it is other than desirable that *The Atheist's Tragedy* – an interesting and, I suspect, if given a suitably sympathetic and daring production, a stage-worthy play in its own right – should be more widely known: it is not a case of either/or, surely, but both.[4]

# Appendix II
# Middleton's Works

I have used Loughrey and Taylor's list in their Penguin edition (1988) as a basis, but have adjusted it where it differs from my own views. An asterisk indicates where doubts have been expressed over Middleton's authorship or involvement, further details of which may usually be found in Lake (1975).

| | |
|---|---|
| 1597 | *The Wisdom of Solomon Paraphrased* (poem) |
| 1599 | *Micro-Cynicon: or Six Snarling Satires* (poems) |
| 1600 | *The Ghost of Lucrece* (poem) |
| 1602 | *Caesar's Fall, or Two Shapes* (lost play, written with Dekker, Drayton, Munday and Webster) |
| 1602 | *The Chester Tragedy, or Randal, Earl of Chester* (lost play) |
| c.1602 | *The Family of Love** (play, written with Dekker) |
| c.1602 | *Blurt, Master Constable** (play) |
| 1603 | *The True Narration of the Entertainment of His Royal Majesty from Edinburgh till London** (pamphlet) |
| 1604 | *The Phoenix* (play) |
| 1604 | *The Honest Whore*, Part One (play, written with, and mainly by, Dekker) |
| 1604 | *Father Hubbard's Tales* (pamphlet) |
| 1604 | *The Black Book* (pamphlet) |
| 1604 | *The Meeting of Gallants at an Ordinary** (pamphlet) |

| 1604-6 | *Michaelmas Term* (play) |
|---|---|
| 1604-6 | *A Mad World, My Masters* (play) |
| 1604-6 | *A Trick to Catch the Old One* (play) |
| 1604-6 | *The Puritan\** (play) |
| 1604-6 | *Your Five Gallants* (play) |
| 1606 | *The Viper and Her Brood* (lost play) |
| 1606-7 | *The Revenger's Tragedy\** (play) |
| 1609 | *The Two Gates of Salvation* (pamphlet) |
| 1609 | *Sir Robert Sherley's Entertainment in Cracovia* (pamphlet) |
| 1611 | *The Second Maiden's Tragedy\** (play) |
| 1611 | *The Roaring Girl* (play, written with Dekker) |
| 1612 | *No Wit, No Help Like a Woman's* (play) |
| 1613 | *A Chaste Maid in Cheapside* (play) |
| 1613 | *Entertainment at the Opening of the New River* (civic pageant) |
| 1613 | *Wit at Several Weapons\** (play, written with Rowley, and possibly Fletcher) |
| 1613 | *The Triumphs of Truth* (Lord Mayor's Show) |
| 1614 | *The Masque of Cupid* (lost masque) |
| c.1614-16 | *The Witch* (play) |
| c.1615 | *More Dissemblers Besides Women* (play) |
| c.1615 | *A Fair Quarrel* (play, written with Rowley) |
| c.1615-16 | *The Widow* (play) |
| c.1616-20 | *The Mayor of Queenborough, or Hengist, King of Kent* (play) |
| 1616 | *Civitatis Amor* (civic pageant) |
| c.1616 | *The Nice Valour\** (play, possibly written with Fletcher) |
| 1617 | *The Triumphs of Honour and Industry* (Lord Mayor's Show) |
| 1618 | *The Peacemaker* (pamphlet) |
| c.1618 | *The Old Law* (play, written with Rowley and possibly Massinger) |
| 1619 | *The Masque of Heroes or The Inner Temple Masque* (masque) |
| 1619 | *Anything for a Quiet Life* (play, written with John Webster) |
| 1619 | *The Triumphs of Love and Antiquity* (Lord Mayor's Show) |

| 1619 | *On the Death of Richard Burbage* (elegy) |
|---|---|
| 1619–20 | *The World Tossed at Tennis* (masque, written with Rowley) |
| 1620–21 | *Honourable Entertainments* (civic entertainments) |
| *c.*1621 | *Women Beware Women* (play) |
| 1621 | *The Sun in Aries* (Lord Mayor's Show, written with Anthony Munday) |
| 1621–3 | *A Match at Midnight\** (play by Rowley, possibly written with Middleton) |
| *c.*1621–7 | *The Puritan Maid, The Modest Wife and The Wanton Widow* (lost play) |
| *c.*1621–7 | *The Conqueror's Custom or The Fair Prisoner* (lost play) |
| 1622 | *The Changeling* (play written with Rowley) |
| 1622 | *An Invention for the Lord Mayor* (private entertainment) |
| 1622 | *The Triumphs of Honour and Virtue* (Lord Mayor's Show) |
| 1623 | *The Triumphs of Integrity* (Lord Mayor's Show) |
| 1623 | *The Spanish Gypsy\** (play, probably by Dekker and Ford, but Middleton has often been claimed as the author, possibly in collaboration with Rowley) |
| 1624 | *A Game at Chess* (play) |
| 1626 | *The Triumphs of Health and Prosperity* (Lord Mayor's Show) |
| 1626 | *Pageant for the Entry of King Charles I and Queen Henrietta Maria* (though after the pageants had been erected the King cancelled the event!) |

David Lake includes the 1608 play, *A Yorkshire Tragedy*, in his list of Middleton collaborations, suggesting the possibility that Shakespeare (named as author in the Stationers' Register) or George Wilkins was the other writer.

# Appendix III
# Tourneur's Works

An asterisk indicates works sometimes attributed to Tourneur, or where the attribution is disputed.

| | |
|---|---|
| 1600 | *The Transformed Metamorphosis* (poem) |
| 1605 | *Laugh and Lie Down** (pamphlet) |
| 1606–7 | *The Revenger's Tragedy** (play) |
| 1609 | *A Funeral Poem on the Death of Sir Francis Vere* (poem) |
| 1611 | *The Atheist's Tragedy* (play) |
| 1612 | *The Nobleman* (lost play) |
| 1612 | *Robert, Earl of Salisbury** (prose 'Character' or portrait) |
| 1613 | *A Grief on the Death of Prince Henry* (poem) |
| c.1613 | *Ye Arraignment of London* (a minor dramatist named Daborne wrote to Philip Henslowe that he had given an act of this play to Tourneur to write but whether Tourneur did the work or whether the play was ever finished or produced is not known.) |

Two further poems, *On the Death of A Child But One Year Old* and *Of My Lady Anne Cecil*, have also been attributed to Tourneur, but their dates of composition are not known.

# Notes

## 1 Middleton's Early Work

1. For more details on Middleton's life see Barker (1958), and Mark Eccles, 'Thomas Middleton A Poett', *Studies in Philology*, LIV (1957) 516–36.

2. References to Middleton's early poetry and prose are to Bullen (1885–6) vol. VIII (1886). *The Phoenix* is printed by Bullen in vol. I. Numbers cited in the text refer to page numbers in Bullen.

3. The term 'Puritan' is a complex and contentious one. Originally applied specifically in a religious sense (and usually abusively), it increasingly acquired during the early decades of the seventeenth century a political and social application. Perhaps some of the meaning the term came to have for contemporaries is revealed in the words of one Mrs Lucy Hutchinson, the wife of a colonel in the Parliamentary army at the time of the Civil War: 'in short, all that crossed the interests of the needy courtiers, the proud encroaching priests, the thievish projectors, the lewd nobility and gentry . . . all these were Puritans' (quoted in Hill, 1980: 90). Heinemann (1982), which explores the connections Middleton's work may have had with 'radical, Parliamentarian or Puritan movements and groupings' (vii) is the most thorough exploration of this aspect of Middleton's work, and Patrick Collinson's short study, *English Puritanism* (1983), published by the Historical Association, is a concise discussion of the subject at large. For a discussion of Calvinism and some implications for Middleton's work see John Stachniewski, 'Calvinist Psychology in Middleton's Tragedies', in Holdsworth (1990: 226–47).

4. *The Ghost of Lucrece*, ed. J. Q. Adams (New York and London, 1937).

5. It has also been suggested that Middleton (alone or with Thomas Dekker) is the author of three other satirical pamphlets – *Plato's Cap*, *News from Gravesend*, and *The Meeting of Gallants at an Ordinary*.

176

6. While this book was being written the remains of the Rose were uncovered in Southwark. The findings of this inestimably important discovery – and its fate – are described in Christine Eccles, *The Rose Theatre* (1990).

7. See Gibbons (1980), Shapiro (1977) and Gair (1982) for more on the Children's companies, and their repertoire and acting style.

8. *The Phoenix*, ed. John Branbury Brooks (New York and London, 1980).

9. David Bergeron (1983: 133) describes Middleton's total output as 'one large morality play'. See also Alan C. Dessen, 'Middleton's *The Phoenix* and the Allegorical Tradition', *Studies in English Literature*, 6 (1966) 291–308.

## 2 City Comedies: *Michaelmas Term, A Mad World, My Masters, A Trick to Catch the Old One*

1. For discussion of the genre of 'city' or 'citizen' comedy, see the works by Leggatt, Gibbons and Leinwand listed in the Bibliography, and Arthur Brown, 'Citizen Comedy and Domestic Drama' in J. R. Brown and Bernard Harris (eds), *Jacobean Theatre*, Stratford-upon-Avon Studies, I (1960) 62–83.

2. For further discussion of what Gibbons calls the 'keen analysis in moral terms' offered by the plays, see L. C. Knights, *Drama and Society in the Age of Jonson* (1982), Leggatt (1973), Gibbons (1980, esp. chs I and II) and Wells (1981).

3. During the period London regularly recorded a greater number of deaths than births, indicating that its rise in population was the result mainly of immigration to the city from the provinces and abroad. Further information on London's expansion and significance can be found in Leinwand (1986) and Pearl (1961). Good introductions to the social, political and artistic background are Briggs (1983), Christopher Hill, *The Century of Revolution 1603–1714*, 2nd edn (Wokingham, 1980), Keith Thomas, *Religion and the Decline of Magic* (1973) ch. 1, 'The Environment', 3–21.

4. Gamini Salgado (ed.), *Cony-Catchers and Bawdy Baskets* (1972) p. 346. Also see Brian Gibbons's useful Appendix, 'A Minor Genre: the Coney-Catching Pamphlet' (1980) 161–7.

5. I have chosen three plays that are Middleton's sole and undisputed authorship. See Appendix II for other plays from this period.

6. Line references are to the edition by Richard Levin in the Regents Renaissance series (University of Nebraska, 1966).

7. Quoted by Levin (1965) xii.

8. R. C. Bald, 'The Sources of Middleton's City Comedies', *Journal of English and Germanic Philology*, 33 (1934) 373–87.

9. Roger Waddrington, *The Tryall and Execution of Father Henry Garnet* (1679); quoted in Gair (1982) 161.

10. In Greek mythology the river Lethe was associated with forgetfulness; Gruel has, of course, 'forgotten' his origins.

11. Line references are to the edition by Standish Henning in the Regents Renaissance Drama Series (University of Nebraska, and London, 1965).

12. A good introduction to this area of study is Kathleen McCluskie's *Renaissance Dramatists*, in the Feminist Readings series (1989). See also Carol Neely, 'Constructing the Subject: Feminist Practice and the New Renaissance Discourses', *English Literary Renaissance*, 18 (1988) 5–18, Loomba (1989), and Malcomson (1990).

13. See also Michael Hattaway's detailed analysis of this speech in 'Drama and Society' in A. R. Braunmuller and Michael Hattaway (eds), *The Cambridge Companion to English Renaissance Drama* (Cambridge, 1990) 122–4. The volume as a whole provides a collection of useful essays on the drama and theatre of the period.

14. Line references are to the edition by G. J. Watson in the New Mermaids series (1968).

15. The Courtesan tells Witgood that 'I have been true unto your pleasure, and all your lands thrice racked, was never worth the jewel which I prodigally gave you, my virginity' (I. i. 33–4). This, however, does not seem to square  with the moment (I. i. 106) when she is recognised by Onesiphorus Hoard, Kix and Limber, as 'evidently a figure of some notoriety in the town' (New Mermaids: 9) which is vital if the ending – when her true identity is revealed to Hoard – is to work.

## 3 *The Roaring Girl*

1. For discussion of the respective contributions of the two authors see Lake (1975) and the Revels edition (Manchester, 1987). The Revels editor, Paul Mulholland, writes that although 'most scenes reveal evidence of both dramatists . . . where plotting threads appear to have antecedents, most derive from Middleton's work – a fair indication that he exercised considerable influence over the structure and shape' (8–12). For the purposes of this discussion I refer to the play as Middleton's. All line references are to the edition by Andor Gomme in the New Mermaids series (1976).

2. See also Orrell (1988).

3. The 'canting' scene (probably Dekker's), V. i., which presents great difficulties to the modern reader or actor, is the most obvious example of this interest, and its (perhaps excessive) length may suggest the writers' awareness of its likely popularity.

4. David Holmes suggests that 'Middleton may have initially intended to involve Greenwit with the Tiltyards in still another plot and then abandoned the idea' (1970: 104–5).

5. See Wright (1935), Rose (1984) and Cherry (1973).

6. *The Chamberlain Letters*, ed. Elizabeth McClure Thomson (1965) 271.

7. See Wright (1935) ch. XIII, 'The Popular Controversy Over

Women' for extracts of these and other pamphlets. Also see Linda Woodbridge, *Women and the English Renaissance: Literature and the Nature of Womankind, 1540–1620* (Urbana, University of Illinois Press, 1984).

## 4  Civic Entertainments
1. Kathleen Dacre, *The People's Theatre of Elizabethan and Jacobean England: 1558–1623*, Ph.D. thesis 1980, University Microfilms International (1988) 278.

## 5  *A Chaste Maid in Cheapside*
1. For further discussion of *A Chaste Maid* at the Swan, see the Revels edition by R. B. Parker (1969) lx–lxvi, and Orrell (1988) for further details of the building. Not all open-air theatres were the same size, and excavations of the Rose revealed a playhouse smaller than estimates for the Swan or the Globe, matching Thomas Dekker's allusion to the Rose in 1599 as 'this small Circumference'. Again this would have influenced acting style: as Christine Eccles (1990: 129) notes, 'Most people who were able to stand on the site in the summer of 1989, exclaimed at its intimacy.'

2. Line references are to the edition by Alan Brissenden in the New Mermaids series (1968).

3. Revels edition, 147–54.

## 6  Tragicomedies: *The Witch* and *A Fair Quarrel*
1. See Lisa Cronin, 'Professional Productions in the British Isles since 1880 of Plays by Tudor and Early Stuart Dramatists (excluding Shakespeare): A Checklist', *Renaissance Drama Newsletter*, Supplement 7, University of Warwick (1987).

2. See also Orrell (1988) especially ch. 12.

3. See Herrick (1955), Hirst (1984), Maguire (1987) and Asp (1974).

4. References are to the edition by Peter Corbin and Douglas Sedge, *Three Jacobean Witchcraft Plays* (Manchester, 1986).

5. See John F. McElroy, *Parody and Burlesque in the Tragicomedies of Thomas Middleton* (Salzburg, 1972).

6. Richard Levin, 'The Two-Audience Theory of English Renaissance Drama', *Shakespeare Studies*, XVIII (1986) 251–75.

7. For details of the divorce and trial see Akrigg (1962: chs XV and XVI), Simmons (1984) and Bromham and Bruzzi (1990).

8. Line references are to the edition by R. V. Holdsworth in the New Mermaids series (1974), whose introduction to the play I have found particularly useful.

9. *A Fair Quarrel* may not be Middleton's only involvement in the issue of duelling; in 1618 a pamphlet entitled *The Peace-Maker, or Great Brittaines Blessing* was entered in the Stationers Register under his name. The pamphlet has also been attributed to Lancelot Andrewes, and some passages have been ascribed to King James himself.

10. F. S. Boas, *An Introduction to Stuart Drama* (Oxford, 1946) 237.

11. Although see Rose (1988) ch. 4, 'Tragicomedy and the Private Life', who argues (p. 182) that Fletcherian tragicomedy is 'too often dismissed as an inward-turning, decadent form' suggesting that on the contrary 'Jacobean tragicomedy can best be understood as participating in an ongoing process of cultural transformation'.

## 7  *The Changeling*

1. See G. E. Bentley, *The Jacobean and Caroline Stage*, vol. I, 182–7.

2. Until recently it was widely believed that a set of drawings held in Worcester College, Oxford, were Inigo Jones's designs for the Phoenix. In 1973 the drawings were dated to the period 1616–18, and in the same year Iain Mackintosh linked them with the Phoenix. In 1977, John Orrell reinforced these proposals in a detailed study ('Inigo Jones at the Cockpit', *Shakespeare Survey*, 30 (1977) 157–68), and in 1985 developed his argument further. A recent thesis by Gordon Higgott, however, challenges the conjectural and circumstantial conclusions of Mackintosh and Orrell by dating the drawings around 1638. John Harris, who first advanced the 1616–18 dating has accepted Higgot's argument, but the reconstruction of the Phoenix that will stand alongside the Globe on the south bank of the Thames will continue to be based on the Worcester College drawings. See John Harris and Gordon Higgot, *Inigo Jones: Complete Architectural Drawings*, catalogue to the Royal Academy Exhibition (1989–90).

3. Line references are to N. C. Bawcutt's Revels edition (Manchester, 1958). After the completion of this book a new edition in the New Mermaids series was published, re-edited by Joost Daalder (1990).

4. William Rowley's date of birth is unknown. Between 1610 and 1617 he was a leading actor with the Prince's Men, and appears to have specialised in 'fat clown' roles, including among his parts Plumporridge in Middleton's *Masque of Heroes* (1619) and the Fat Bishop in *A Game at Chess* (1624), by which time it appears he was a member of the King's Men. As a playwright he produced few plays independently, but in collaboration with other writers produced some of the period's finest plays. He often created parts suitable for himself to play, such as that of Cuddy Banks in *The Witch of Edmonton*, which he wrote with Thomas Dekker and John Ford in 1621. In *A Fair Quarrel*, his first collaboration with Middleton, it seems likely that he not only wrote, but acted, the part of Chough. It appears he died in 1626.

5. The principal source is a story in the first of the six books that make up John Reynold's *The Triumphs of God's Revenge against the Crying and Execrable Sin of Wilful and Premeditated Murder*, published in 1621. See the Revels edition for a discussion of this and other sources and for extracts from Reynolds, and see Bromham and Bruzzi (1990) for further views on the relationship of source and play.

6. For discussion of the naming of characters see William Power, 'Middleton's Way with Names', *Notes and Queries* (1960) 205. Although

Middleton and Rowley took the majority of the characters' names in *The Changeling* from the source, their 'meanings' are highly appropriate. In particular, Dale Randall notes that while '"Beatrice", meaning she who makes happy or blessed . . . suggests all that Beatrice-Joanna appears to be. . . . "Joanna" . . . had by the sixteenth century become one of the commonest of English names and apparently fallen to the kitchen and the cottage', and she sees it as a double name which may be intended to reflect the sense of two aspects of a personality in conflict, rather than being 'a merely borrowed label' (1984: 352).

  7. Interestingly, I think, the *lamia* figures in a story recounted by Robert Burton in *The Anatomy of Melancholy*, which was published in 1621, a year before the play was written, and which enjoyed enormous popularity. Burton gives the story as one among many examples of the 'power and extent' of love. The story tells of a young man who meets and falls for a 'fair gentlewoman' who promises him she will 'live and die with him'. Burton continues: 'The young man, a philosopher, otherwise staid and discreet, able to moderate his passions, though not this of love, tarried with her awhile to his great content, and at last married her, to whose wedding, amongst other guests came Appolonius, who, by some probable conjectures, found her out to be a serpent, a lamia, and that all her furniture was like Tantalus's gold described by Homer, no substance, but mere illusions. When she saw herself descried, she wept, and desired Appollonius to be silent, but he would not be moved, and thereupon she, plate, house, and all that was in it, vanished in an instance.' While not wishing to offer this as a direct source, in the presentation of a 'staid and discreet' hero, not dissimilar to Alsemero, whose senses are deceived when overruled by desire, the emphasis on the illusion of appearances, the revelation of the desired one's 'true' nature, and in the connections the 'serpent' has with the imagery of Eden and the Fall with which Alsemero opens the play, Burton's tale seems to me to touch on issues and images central to the play. I have not seen this possible connection mentioned elsewhere. See Robert Burton, *The Anatomy of Melancholy*, 3 vols (1893) vol. III, 11–12. See also John Stachniewski, 'Calvinist Psychology in Middleton's Tragedies', in Holdsworth (1990) 226–47, p. 229; and Bromham and Bruzzi (1990) for further discussion of the contemporary interest in 'changelings'.

  8. As De Flores exits to the closet where Beatrice-Joanna is, Alsemero tells him to 'rehearse again/Your scene of lust' (V. iii. 114–15). Ann Pasternak Slater suggests that until De Flores enters with the bleeding body of Beatrice-Joanna, the audience cannot know whether her cries are of orgasm or distress ('Hypallage, Barley-Break, and *The Changeling*', *Review of English Studies*, vol. XXXIV (1983) 429–40. This echoes III. ii. of *A Mad World, My Masters*, where Harebrain believes the off-stage cries of his wife are the sounds of her weeping, whereas she is in fact making love to Penitent Brothel (see p. 37 above).

  9. See Pentzell (1986). Pentzell's excellent essay makes a range of

points that are generally applicable to Middleton's work, and to *The Revenger's Tragedy*.

10. For a rather different interpretation of Alsemero's and Vermandero's responses to Beatrice-Joanna's death, see John Stachniewski, 'Calvinist Psychology'.

11. See Bromham and Bruzzi (1990: esp. ch. 1), and Simmons (1984); also see chapter 6 above.

12. One of the play's sources, Leonard Digges's *Gerardo The Unfortunate Spaniard* (in which a subsitute is used on a wedding night and then murdered), was not entered in the Stationers' Register until 11 March 1622, indicating that *The Changeling* must have been written, at least in part, in the short time between then and 7 May when the play was licensed.

## 8 *Women Beware Women*

1. Heinemann (1982); see Bromham and Bruzzi (1990) for a discussion of the relationship of *More Dissemblers* (which they date at 1619) to contemporary political events.

2. Line references are to Ronald Mulryne's Revels edition (Manchester, 1975).

3. G. E. Rowe suggests that Middleton's frequent use of games in imagery and action in his plays may reflect his portrayal of a 'society in which a universal pursuit of pleasure leads to a cynical disregard for all conventional moral codes' (1979: 195), while Loughrey and Taylor believe it may also have provided him with 'a powerful metaphor for the Calvinist conception of life as being strict, competitive and teleological' (1988: xx).

4. In 1606, for example, during the celebrations to mark the visit of Christian IV, King James's brother-in-law, an entertainment was provided which, mainly because the majority of those taking part were drunk, turned into a complete shambles. For Sir John Harington the disarray was symbolic of the difference between Elizabeth's court and that of James, since 'in our Queen's days . . . I neer did see such lack of good order, discretion, and sobriety, as I have now done' (Ashton, 1969: 244).

5. See Inga-Stina Ekblad's useful discussion of the appropriateness of the masque in 'A Study of Masques in Plays' in T. J. B. Spencer and S. W. Wells (eds), *A Book of Masques* (Cambridge, 1967), and Leslie Thomson, '"Enter Above": The Staging of *Women Beware Women*', *Studies in English Literature*, 26 (1986) 331–43.

6. *Women Beware Women* by Thomas Middleton and Howard Barker (1986). The production, directed by William Gaskill, opened at the Royal Court Theatre, London, in Spring 1986.

## 9 *A Game at Chess*

1. See Robin Clifton, 'Fear of Popery', in Conrad Russell (ed.), *The Origins of the English Civil War* (1973) 144–67.

2. *The Second Maiden's Tragedy*, ed. Anne Lancashire (Manchester, 1978). The edition includes detailed discussion of the play's authorship and its religious/political attitudes, and draws attention to the links between it and Middleton's poem *The Wisdom of Solomon Paraphrased* (see chapter 1). The Introduction also throws light on the authorship of *The Revenger's Tragedy*. Also see Clare (1990) 158–65, for further information on the censorship of the play.

3. *The Mayor of Queenborough or Hengist, King of Kent*, ed. R. C. Bald (Amherst, Mass., 1938).

4. *The World Tossed at Tennis*, in Bullen (1886) vol. VII, ll. 875–6.

5. For a discussion of the relationship of Middleton's later plays to contemporary issues see Bromham and Bruzzi (1990: ch. 5).

6. *The Diary of Sir Simonds D'Ewes*, ed. J. O. Halliwell, 2 vols (1845) vol. I, 238.

7. 'Arminians' were originally followers of the anti-Calvinist Dutch theologian Jacobus Arminius. In England, under the leadership of William Laud, who stressed the ritual of worship, the movement became equated by many with crypto-catholicism. Useful material on the religious and political background is provided by Dures (1983) and Houston (1973). See also Roussel Sargent, 'Theme and Structure in Middleton's *A Game at Chess*', *Modern Language Review*, lxvi (October 1971) 721–30; Louis B. Wright, 'Propaganda against James I's "Appeasement" of Spain', *Huntington Library Quarterly*, VI (1942–3) 149–72; and T. H. Howard-Hill, 'The Origins of Middleton's *A Game at Chess*', *Research Opportunities in Renaissance Drama*, XXVIII (1985) 3–14.

8. Line references are to the edition by J. W. Harper in the New Mermaids edition, 1966.

9. In a series of practical classes on the play it became clear that the chess scenes benefit from appropriately 'formal' staging, while the Pawns' plot, an exciting sexual intrigue, is remarkably lively and often very comic. The fact that it, like the Govianus/Lady plot in *The Second Maiden's Tragedy*, has an 'allegorical' dimension does not mean that it is necessarily less attractive or successful theatrically, and it should be remembered that the allegorical sections of plays are also being communicated through actors with distinctive shapes, voices, and personalities.

10. All contemporary references to the play's presentation and reception can be found in R. C. Bald's edition (Cambridge, 1929). See also A. R. Braunmuller, '"To the Globe I rowed": John Holles Sees *A Game at Chess*', *ELR*, 20 (1990) 340–56, for details of an eye-witness account of the play

# 10  Thomas Middleton: Summary and Conclusions

1. See Ricks (1960, 1961) for a particularly fine analysis of Middleton's language.

2. John F. McElroy, 'Middleton, Entertainer or Moralist? An

Interpretation of *The Family of Love* and *Your Five Gallants'*, *Modern Language Quarterly*, 37 (1976) 35–46.

3. It is in this combination of engagement and detachment that many critics have identified a similarity between Middleton and Brecht. As Jonathan Dollimore observes: 'Brecht's own notion of "epic" theatre was derived in part from the Elizabethans and Jacobeans, especially the emphasis on contradiction and struggle, these corresponding directly to the struggles and contradictions within the society which the theatre re-presents: between individuals, within individuals, between classes, between dominant and emergent social groups' ('Middleton and Barker: Creative Vandalism', a note to Howard Barker's *Women Beware Women*, 1986). See also Gibbons (1980) 6–8.

4. Quoted by Sara Jayne Steen, 'The Response to Middleton: His Own Time to Eliot', *Research Opportunities in Renaissance Drama*, XXVII (1985) 63–85. The volume contains other essays dealing with Middleton's plays.

## 11 *The Revenger's Tragedy*

1. See Bowers (1966), Peter (1956) and Salingar (1938).

2. Line references are to Brian Gibbons's New Mermaids edition (1967).

3. See Gibbons's edition for further thoughts on and illustrations of contemporary emblematic imagery related to the play.

4. William Archer, *The Old Drama and the New* (1923) 73, 75.

5. Cyrus Hoy, 'Shakespeare's Mannerist Style', in *Shakespeare Survey*, 26 (1973) 49–67, p. 49.

6. Thomas Nashe, *The Unfortunate Traveller*, ed. J. B. Steane (1972) 345.

7. See Inga-Stina Ewbank (Ekeblad), 'An Approach to Tourneur's Imagery', *Modern Language Review*, LIV (1959) 489–98.

8. Larry S. Champion, *Studies in Philology*, 72 (1975) 299–321, p. 312, calculates that Vindice delivers seven soliloquies and forty asides with a total of 201 lines (nineteen fewer than Hamlet), which are concentrated most heavily in the first two acts.

9. See the comments on the Jacobean masque and its use in plays, and other works referred to, in chapter 8, *Women Beware Women*.

10. Philip Thomson, *The Grotesque* (1972) p. 11.

11. *Hamlet*, III. ii. 244.

## 12 *The Atheist's Tragedy, or The Honest Man's Revenge*

1. R. J. Kaufmann, 'Theodicy, Tragedy, and the Psalmist: Tourneur's *Atheist's Tragedy*', in C. Davidson *et al.* (eds), *Drama in the Renaissance* (New York, 1986).

2. Richard Levin, 'The Subplot of *The Atheist's Tragedy*', *Huntington Library Quarterly*, 29 (1965) 17–33.

3. For discussion of the genre of revenge tragedy, see Bowers (1966).

4. See Inga-Stina Ewbank, 'An Approach to Tourneur's Imagery'.

5. Kaufman, 'Theodicy, Tragedy, and the Psalmist', 210, 213.

6. The production ran at the Belgrade Theatre, Coventry, from 22 March until 7 April 1979, and was directed by Ed Thomason. A generally unfavourable review in *Research Opportunities in Renaissance Drama*, 22 (1979) 83, laid the blame not on the play itself but on the director's failure to address the problem of 'presenting a general audience with ethical problems couched in specifically 17th century terms', a problem that, indeed, frequently confronts directors, designers and actors of Jacobean plays.

7. Quoted by J. A. Symonds in his Introduction to the Mermaid *Webster and Tourneur* (1959 reprint) p. 7.

## Appendix I

1. G. R. Price, 'The Authorship and the Bibliography of *The Revenger's Tragedy*', *The Library*, 5th Series, 15 (1960) 262–70; M. P. Jackson, *Studies in Attribution: Middleton and Shakespeare* (Salzburg, 1979); Lake (1975); Murray (1964).

2. Samuel Schoenbaum, *Internal Evidence and Elizabethan Dramatic Authorship* (1966) 213.

3. Anne Lancashire (ed.), *The Second Maiden's Tragedy* (Manchester, 1978). Lancashire's points are not advanced specifically in order to suggest Middleton as the author of *The Revenger's Tragedy*.

4. See chapter 12, and n. 6 to that chapter.

# Select Bibliography

Further bibliograhical information can be found in Dorothy Wolff, *Thomas Middleton: An Annotated Bibliography* (New York, 1985), and in John B. Brooks, 'Recent Studies in Middleton', *English Literary Renaissance [ELR]*, 14 (1984), 114–28. The place of publication is London unless otherwise stated.

Akrigg, G. P. V. (1962), *Jacobean Pageant*.

Anderson, Ruth Leila (1964), *Elizabethan Psychology and Shakespeare's Plays*, New York.

Ashton, Robert (ed.) (1969), *James I By His Contemporaries*.

Asp, Caroline (1974), *A Study of Thomas Middleton's Tragicomedies*, Salzburg.

Ayres, Philip J. (1977), *Tourneur: The Revenger's Tragedy*.

Barker, R. H. (1958), *Thomas Middleton*, New York.

Bergeron, David M. (1971), *English Civic Pageantry, 1558–1642*.

Bergeron, David M. (1983), 'Middleton's Moral Landscape: *A Chaste Maid in Cheapside* and *The Triumphs of Truth*', in Friedenreich, *'Accompaninge the Players'*, 133–46.

Bowers, Fredson (1966), *Elizabethan Revenge Tragedy 1587–1642*, Princeton, NJ, first published 1940.

Bradbrook, Muriel (1966), *Themes and Conventions of Elizabethan Tragedy*, Cambridge, first published 1935.

Bradbrook, Muriel (1981), 'The Politics of Pageantry: Social Implications in Jacobean London', in Antony Coleman and Antony Hammond (eds), *Poetry and Drama 1570–1700*.

Briggs, Julia (1983), *This Stage-Play World*, Oxford.

Bristol, M. (1985), *Carnival and Theatre: Plebeian Culture and the Structure of Authority in Renaissance England*.

Bromham, A. A. (1986), 'The Tragedy of Peace: Political Meaning in *Women Beware Women*', *Studies in English Literature*, vol. 26, 309–43.

Bromham, A. A. and Bruzzi, Zara (1990), *The Changeling and the Years of Crisis 1619–1624: a Hieroglyph of Britain*.

Brooke, Nicholas (1979), *Horrid Laughter in Jacobean Tragedy*.

Bullen, A. H. (ed.) (1885–6), *The Works of Thomas Middleton*, 8 vols.

Chatterji, Ruby (1965), 'Theme, Imagery and Unity in *A Chaste Maid in Cheapside*', *Renaissance Drama*, vol. VIII, 105–26.

Chatterji, Ruby (1968), 'Unity and Disparity in *Michaelmas Term*', *Studies in English Literature*, vol. VIII, 349–63.

Cherry, Caroline Lockett (1973), *The Most Unvaluedst Purchase: Women in The Plays of Thomas Middleton*, Salzburg.

Clare, Janet (1990), *'Art made tongue-tied by authority': Elizabethan and Jacobean Dramatic Censorship*, Manchester.

Daalder, Joost (1988), 'Folly and Madness in *The Changeling*', *Essays in Criticism*, vol. 38, 1–19.

Dessen, Alan (1985), *Elizabethan Stage Conventions and Modern Interpreters*, Cambridge.

Dollimore, J. (1984), *Radical Tragedy: Religion, Ideology and Power in the Drama of Shakespeare and his Contemporaries*, Brighton.

Dures, Alan (1983), *English Catholicism 1558–1642*, Harlow.

Eliot, T. S. (1963), *Elizabethan Dramatists*.

Ewbank, Inga-Stina (1969), 'Realism and Morality in *Women Beware Women*', *Essays and Studies*, vol. 22, 57–70.

Farley-Hills, David (1988), *Jacobean Drama*.

Farr, Dorothy M. (1973), *Thomas Middleton and the Drama of Realism*.

Foakes, R. A. (1970), 'Tragedy at the Children's Theatres after 1600: A Challenge to the Adult Stage', *The Elizabethan Theatre II*, ed. David Galloway, Toronto, 37–59.

Foakes, R. A. (1978), 'On Marston, *The Malcontent*, and *The Revenger's Tragedy*', *The Elizabethan Theatre VI*, ed. David Galloway, Toronto, 59–75.

Foakes, R. A. (1985), *Illustrations of the English Stage 1580–1642*.

Friedenreich, Kenneth (ed.) (1983), *'Accompaninge the Players': Essays Celebrating Thomas Middleton, 1580–1980*, New York.

Gair, W. Reavley (1982), *The Children of Paul's: The Story of a Theatre Company, 1553–1608*, Cambridge.

Gibbons, Brian (1980), *Jacobean City Comedy*, first published 1968.

Gill, Roma (1983), 'The World of Thomas Middleton', in Friedenreich, *'Accompaninge the Players'*, 15–38.

Gurr, Andrew (1970), *The Shakespearian Stage 1574–1642*, Cambridge.

Gurr, Andrew (1987), *Playgoing in Shakespeare's London*, Cambridge.

Haller, William and Haller, Malleville (1941–2), 'The Puritan Art of Love', *Huntington Library Quarterly*, vol. V, 235–72.

Heinemann, Margot (1982), *Puritanism and Theatre: Thomas Middleton and Opposition Drama under the Early Stuarts*, Cambridge, first published 1980.

Herrick, Marvin T. (1955), *Tragicomedy: Its Origin and Development in Italy, France, and England*, University of Illinois, Urbana.

Hill, Christopher (1980), *The Century of Revolution*, first published 1961.

Hill, Christopher (1985), 'Censorship and English Literature', in *The Collected Essays of Christopher Hill*, vol. I, Brighton.

Hirst, David (1984), *Tragicomedy*.

Holdsworth, R. V. (ed.) (1990), *Three Jacobean Revenge Tragedies*, Casebook Series.

Holmes, David M. (1970), *The Art of Thomas Middleton: A Critical Study*.

Houston, S. J. (1973), *James I*, Harlow.

Howard, Jean E. (1988), 'Crossdressing, the Theatre, and Gender Struggle in Early Modern England', *Shakespeare Quarterly*, vol. 39 (Winter) no. 4, 418–40.

Jardine, Lisa (1983), *Still Harping on Daughters: Women and Drama in the Age of Shakespeare*, Brighton.

Knights, L. C. (1962), *Drama and Society in the Age of Jonson*, first published 1937.

Lake, D. J. (1975), *The Canon of Thomas Middleton's Plays: Internal Evidence for the Major Problems of Authorship*, Cambridge.

Lancashire, Anne (1983), '*The Witch*: Stage Flop or Political Mistake?', in Friedenreich '*Accompaninge the Players*', 161–81.

Leggatt, Alexander (1973), *Jacobean Citizen Comedy in the Age of Shakespeare*, Toronto.

Leggatt, Alexander (1988), *English Drama: Shakespeare to the Restoration, 1590–1660*.

Leinwand, Theodore B. (1986), *The City Staged: Jacobean Comedy 1603–1613*, Madison, Wis.

Lever, J. W. (1987), *The Tragedy of State*, Manchester, first published 1971.

Levin, Richard (1965), 'The Four Plots of *A Chaste Maid in Cheapside*', *Review of English Studies*, n.s., vol. XVI, 14–24.

Limon, Jerzy (1986), *Dangerous Matter: English Drama and Politics in 1623/24*, Cambridge.

Lisca, Peter (1959), '*The Revenger's Tragedy*: a Study in Irony', *Philological Quarterly*, vol. XXXVIII, 242–51.

Loomba, Ania (1989), *Gender, Race, Renaissance Drama*.

Loughrey, Bryan, and Taylor, Neil (eds) (1988), *Thomas Middleton: Five Plays*.

Maguire, Nancy Klein (ed.) (1987), *Renaissance Tragi-Comedy*, New York.

Malcomson, Christina (1990) '"As Tame as the Ladies": Politics and Gender in *The Changeling*', *ELR*, vol. 20, 320–39.

Mehl, D. (1965), *The Elizabethan Dumb Show*.

Mooney, Michael E. (1983), '"This Luxurious Circle": Figurenposition in *The Revenger's Tragedy*', *ELR*, vol. 13, 162–81.

Mulryne, J. R. (1979), *Thomas Middleton*, Harlow.

Murray, Peter B. (1964), *A Study of Cyril Tourneur*, Philadelphia.

Nagler, A. M. (1959), *A Sourcebook in Theatrical History*, New York.

Orgel, Stephen (1975), *The Illusion of Power: Political Theater in the English Renaissance*, Berkeley, Calif.

Ornstein, Robert (1965), *The Moral Vision of Jacobean Tragedy*, Madison, Wis.

Orrell, John (1988), *The Human Stage: English Theatre Design, 1576–1640*, Cambridge.

Parker, R. B. (1960), 'Middleton's Experiments with Comedy and Judgement', *Jacobean Theatre*, ed. J. R. Brown and B. Harris, Stratford-upon-Avon Studies, vol. I, 179–99.

Pearl, Valerie (1961), *London and the Outbreak of the Puritan Revolution*, Oxford.

Pentzell, Raymond J. (1986), '*The Changeling*: Notes on Mannerism in Dramatic Form', in Clifford Davidson, G. J. Gianakaris and John H. Stroupe (eds), *Drama in the Renaissance*, New York, 274–99.

Peter, John (1956), *Complaint and Satire in Early English Literature*, Oxford.

Randall, Dale B. J. (1984), 'Some Observations on the Theme of Chastity in *The Changeling*', *ELR*, vol. 14, 347–66.

Ricks, Christopher (1960), 'The Moral and Poetic Structure of *The Changeling*', *Essays in Criticism*, vol. 10, 290–306.

Ricks, Christopher (1961), 'Word Play in *Women Beware Women*', *Review of English Studies*, n.s., vol. 12, 238–50.

Rose, Mary Beth (1984), 'Women in Men's Clothing: Apparel and Social Stability in *The Roaring Girl*', *ELR*, vol. 14, 367–91.

Rose, Mary Beth (1988), *The Expense of Spirit: Love and Sexuality in English Drama*, Ithaca, NY.

Rowe, George E. (1979), *Thomas Middleton and the New Comedy Tradition*, Lincoln, Nebr.

Salingar, L. G. (1938), '*The Revenger's Tragedy* and the Morality Tradition', *Scrutiny*, vol. VI, 402–22.

Schoenbaum, Samuel (1956), 'Middleton's Tragicomedies', *Modern Philology*, vol. 54, 7–19.

Schoenbuam, Samuel (1959), '*A Chaste Maid in Cheapside* and Middleton's City Comedy', in J. W. Bennett, O. Cargill and V. Hall (eds), *Studies in the English Renaissance Drama*, 287–309.

Schoenbaum, Samuel (1970), *Middleton's Tragedies*, New York, first published 1955.

Seaver, Paul S. (1985), *Wallington's World: A Puritan Artisan in Seventeenth-century London*.

Shand, G. B. (1983), 'The Elizabethan Aim of *The Wisdom of Solomon Paraphrased*', in Friedenreich, '*Accompaninge the Players*', 67,19677.

Shand, G. B. (1985), 'The Stagecraft of *Women Beware Women*', *Research Opportunities in Renaissance Drama*, vol. XXVIII, 29–36.

Shapiro, Michael (1977), *Children of the Revels: the Boy Companies of Shakespeare's Time and Their Plays*, New York.

Shepherd, S. (1981), *Amazons and Warrior Women: Varieties of Feminism in Seventeenth Century Drama*, Brighton.

Sherman, Jane (1978), 'The Pawn's Allegory in Middleton's *A Game At Chesse*', *Review of English Studies*, vol. 29, 147–59.

Simmons, J. L. (1980), 'Diabolical Realism in Middleton and Rowley's *The Changeling*', *Renaissance Drama*, n.s., vol. XI, 135–70.

Slade, Giles (1989), 'The City as an Image of Social Dialogue in Jacobean Comedy', *Essays in Theatre*, vol. 8, no. 1 (November) 61–6.

Sontag, Susan (1983), *A Sontag Reader*.

Stonex, A. B. (1916), 'The Usurer in Elizabethan Drama', *Publications of the Modern Languages Association*, vol. XXXI, 190–210.

Sturgess, Keith (1987), *Jacobean Private Theatre*.

Taylor, Neil, and Loughrey, Brian (1984), 'Middleton's Chess Strategies in *Women Beware Women*', *Studies in English Literature*, vol. 24, 341–54.

Thomas, Keith (1977), 'The Place of Laughter in Tudor and Stuart England', *The Times Literary Supplement*, 21 January, 76–81.

Thomson, Peter (1983), *Shakespeare's Theatre*.

Tydeman, William (1985), 'The Image of the City in English Renaissance Drama', *Essays and Studies*, vol. 38, 29–44.

Wells, Susan (1981), 'Jacobean City Comedy and the Ideology of the City', *English Literary History*, vol. 48, 37–60.

Wharton, T. F. (1988), *Moral Experiment in Jacobean Drama*.

Williamson, Hugh Ross (1940), *George Villiers, First Duke of Buckingham*.

Willson, D. H. (1971), *King James VI and I*.

Wright, Louis B. (1935), *Middle-Class Culture in Elizabethan England*, Chapel Hill, NC.

Yanchin, Paul (1982), '*A Game At Chess* and Chess Allegory', *Studies in English Literature*, vol. 22, 317–30.

# Index